D1707039

1

This book is historical fiction. Most of the events are true, however to make this timeline realistic, King David had to hold on to power using force.

I would like to give a special thanks to my editor Amy, and my illustrator Grace. Plus a special thank you to Debi, Mike, and Michelle from their support. Lastly, a big mahalo to Mark, Ingrid, and Jeff for their insight and inspiration.

I wrote this book because I love history and I love Hawai'i.

Hawaiian State II, A Story of Queen Lydia Kamaka'eha

Hawaiian State III, A Story of Maili, the Pebble Queen

Hawaiian State IV, A Story of the Twin Queens of Hawai'i

Hawaiian State

A Story of King David Kalākaua

Hawaiian State

A Story of King David Kalakaua

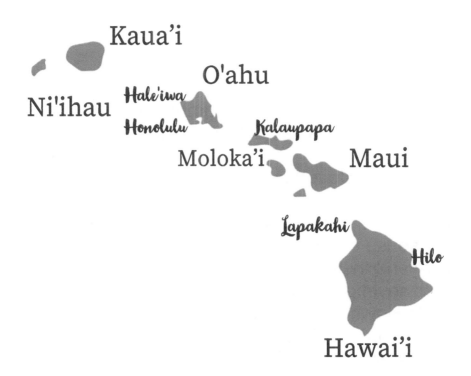

Kaua'i

O'ahu

Ni'ihau   Hale'iwa

Honolulu   Kalaupapa

Moloka'i   Maui

Lapakahi

Hilo

Hawai'i

J. Chamberlain

Praise for J. Chamberlain's
Hawaiian State series

"We are privileged to have students from across the Pacific here at Kaiser High School. We need more stories like these to help my students feel that sense of belonging. My students enjoyed the story and they are happier than any other time! Your novel gave me the green light to implement 'Olelo Hawai'i' mini-lessons which I love and so do my students."
   -Ingrid Vasilescu, English Teacher, Henry Kaiser High School
Honolulu, Hawai'i

"The book series is fascinating, informative and a must read for anyone interested in learning about the history of the Hawaiian Islands. A great read for children and adults. Each book will keep you hooked and wanting more."

-Marcie Dougals, English Teacher, Joseph Kerr Middle School
Elk Grove, California

"Read the first of the series on my trip to Hawai'i. After reading it I couldn't wait to read the second one because I wanted to recall the historical events in the books. After reading book two, I am eager to read book three."

-Terry Page, Engineer
Star, Idaho

"Whether you enjoy Hawai'i, history, or both, J. Chamberlain did a wonderful job describing Hawai'i, along with additional storylines and characters. As someone who enjoys Hawai'i, I found this serves as a delightful way to learn about Hawai'i's past. I believe this series is appropriate reading for middle school to college aged students, and intriguing for Asian Pacific Islanders, as well as those who just love Hawai'i."

-Terra Beaudin, Elementary Teacher, Elk Grove Elementary
Elk Grove, California

"It's engaging, historical, and keeps you wanting to read more. An easy read for all ages."

-Jaden Martin

Cleveland, Tennessee

"Having lived and continued making sojourns back "home", I was impressed with the amount of time Mr. Chamberlain spent researching for his historical fiction book *"Hawaiian State"*. Moloka'i is a special place and he definitely captured the "Friendly Island's" place in Hawaiian lore."
    -Jeffrey Wise, Educator, Riles Middle School, Antelope, CA
    Kaunakakai, Kalae, Moloka'i, Hawai'i

"Hawaiian State is a work of historical fiction that I would highly recommend to anyone interested in Hawaiian culture. The author integrates events from history with a beautiful story of a fictional heir to the Hawaiian throne. It is very entertaining and an easy read."
    -Emily Aksamit, Educator, B.S. in Creative Writing, UCSB
    Lincoln, Nebraska

Introduction

The history of the Hawaiian language is as controversial as the history of Hawai'i itself. The origins of the Hawaiian language go back to ancient Polynesia.

The oral traditions of the early Hawaiians made it difficult for the early missionaries of the 1800s to translate and create an alphabet due to irregularities among the separate islands.

For example, the first westerner to visit the Hawaiian Islands was Captain Cook in 1778. The Chief of Moloka'i pronounced Morota'i, according to Cook's journal. Somehow, that evolved into Moloka'i. Moreover, depending on who you talk to on Moloka'i today, some islanders pronounce it Molokai, and some pronounce it Moloka'i.

The ability of the Hawaiian language to expand between the Hawaiians and the missionaries was expedited by a little know Hawaiian mariner known as Obookiah. He was largely responsible for spreading Christianity and literacy by educating missionaries from New England on the Hawaiian language.

As the missionaries attempted to create an alphabet and dictionary, they found the Hawaiians to have only five vowels (a,e,i,o,u), eight consonants (h,k,l,m,n,p,w), and a glottal stop that has an 'okina to tell when to break up the vowel sounds. However, not all double vowels have an okina.

As the years passed in the 1800's, the Hawaiian population was decimated by disease, and thousands of foreigners from around the world flooded the islands, introducing their languages. As people do, they adapt. Some might argue that the Hawaiian language was high jacked by foreigners.

Pidgin was created out of necessity for all of the mixed languages working on the plantations. Hawaiians speak today with the influences of Native Hawaiian words, University Hawaiian, and Pidgin.

In addition, Hawaiian Mō'ī often had many names and nicknames. There is confusion on what the accurate names of the Mō'ī, or monarchy. For example, Queen Lydia's birth name is Lydia Lili'u Loku Walania Wewehi Kamake'eha. She was given the name Lydia after she was baptized by Reverend Levi

Chamberlain when she was two months old. Also, she was adopted early by Abner Paki to keep with the elite Hawaiian family tradition. So in early life, people added Paki to her name.

Eventually, she would be known as Queen Lili'oukalani. For consistency in the book, she will have that name as well as Queen Lydia.

As modern-day Hawaiians yearn to reconnect to their ancient roots, this story will use more of the traditional spelling of many Hawaiian words and islands. However, in conversation, you may find English-speaking characters using their style of Hawaiian interpretation.

Chapter 1
Princess Maili,
Shipwreck Beach, Poipu, Kaua'i – June 15, 1899

She was named Princess Maili Grace Baitmen Kaanapali. Maili carefully walked towards the cliff's edge. Even though it was early in the morning, the sun radiated intense tropical heat. Maili shuffled slowly to the edge of the cliff with her knees bent. She had her wrists cocked at a right angle away from her body. She slowly and carefully walked as far out on the point as she could go. She wasn't wearing her traditional gown. She was wearing a modern white dress sprinkled with vibrant blue flowers. Her long, black, wavy hair was pulled off her face by her royal *lole po'o*, or haku. As she slowly approached the point, she looked down and to the left. Maili was desperately trying to catch a glimpse of The Forbidden Cave. Maili slid one step closer to the point of the cliff.

Elizabeth Doel was right behind her. Lizzy, as Maili called her, had just turned nine. She was a few months older than Princess Maili. Many years ago, Lizzy's father Kenneth had saved the king's life. This act promoted the Doel family into the king's inner circle, and paved the way for the girls to become best friends.

Lizzy's eyes were locked on the princess. Falling off the cliff was almost certain death. The girls had been told not to go near the Menehune Cave, and to stay away from the cliffs. Lizzy knew she'd be blamed if anything were to happen to the princess.

Looking over the edge, Maili could see sand, jagged coral, and sharp sandstone peaking through the surf. Even though there were no storms nearby, the waves below were large and slowly rolling onto the rocks. As if in slow motion, they would grow in size, then violently crash onto the rocks. The power of these waves sprayed the ocean halfway up the cliff. The sea spray made its way up to the girls. They could smell and taste the salty ocean. The water was a brilliant turquoise, and it kept catching Maili's attention.

Just a few feet behind her, Lizzy was wearing a traditional Hawaiian gown for missionary girls. It was dragging on the ground; her anxiety rose every time the hemline got snagged on a rock. Her vision was partially blocked by her long, golden brown hair. It whipped her face as the wind gusts swirled around them.

The girls were not aware the cliff they were standing on had been carved away underneath from centuries of endless waves wearing down the soft sandstone.

Down on the beach, about fifty yards away, were two boys about the same age as the girls. Hideki Yamamoto was allowed to go fishing on Saturdays if his chores were complete. Hideki had recently purchased the best fishing gear he could afford. He had worked for weeks to pay for the pole. Hideki was with his Chinese servant, Po San. If the chores weren't done, he could easily blame Po San, and Po San would take the belt in his stead. Even so, Po San went where Hideki went; they were always together.

Hideki was born in Japan and retained his Japanese accent, "Hey Po, look at those stupid girls up on the point. Why would you go out so far? I bet you a pineapple one of them falls off."

Po San had a strong accent as well, as he had not lived in Hawai'i very long. He laughed and replied, " Ha, I bet you a coconut! Hey Hideki, what's the biggest fish you've ever caught?"

"Well once I snagged a turtle. It must have been 50 pounds. I got really mad. My hook snagged his flipper, and I had to go out and try to unhook it. That stupid turtle just kept swimming, so I cut my line. But a real fish, hmmmm, I caught a ten pound mahimahi. Man that thing really fought. It almost broke my pole!"

Suddenly up on the point, Lizzy heard a loud CRACK and the earth shook. Lizzy fell on her bottom and crawled backwards like a crab on her hands and feet as fast as she could. "PRINCESS!" she screamed.

The princess turned frantically, looked into Lizzy's eyes with terror, and then disappeared!

Hideki and Po gasped as they saw the girl fall nearly fifty feet into the surf. Hideki yelled at Po to run to the village to get help. It was nearly a half a mile away. Po ran incredibly fast, and this unique skill gave him much joy. He'd walk out a front door, and as fast as he could, run around to the back of the house and pretend to be his own twin. Po ran all the time. Running a half a mile to the village took him only three minutes.

Hideki was in incredible shape for turning just ten years old. He was an excellent swimmer, but even he knew this was a stupid thing to do. He ran as fast as he could until he reached the large swells. He struggled to get to deep enough water until a large wave rose in front of him. Hideki dove under the wave and swam until he could see the cliff's rubble. The ocean water always stung his eyes at first, but he was used to it after years of swimming in the warm Pacific. Climbing out of the water he looked for the girl. He heard a faint scream from above. It was Lizzy. Her face was just visible leaning over the edge.

Faintly he heard, "Over there!" Lizzy pointed just feet away.

Hideki saw the girl's *haku, or lole po'o* floating away. He realized only royalty wore those types of crowns. Without warning another large swell knocked him off the rocks. The wave smashed him on to the rocks and coral. He was scraped badly all over the left side of his body. However he quickly stood up again. The girl was laying face down floating near the rocks. The next swell was approaching. Hideki grabbed the girl and braced himself with his feet towards the cliff. A sudden movement near the opening of the cave caught his eye. He hoped for a second that someone had come to help. However, a huge wave splashed over them, and the saltwater stung badly all over his new abrasions. He looked back into the cave, but whatever caught his eyes was gone. Hideki grabbed the girl and slowly swam her to the beach.

As Hideki was dragging the princess to the beach, several *kanes*, village men, ran down to assist. The royal guard arrived first and pushed Hideki out of the way. "Get out of the way *keiki!* What have you done? Do you know who this is? You will go to prison if she is hurt!"

Hideki was exhausted and breathing heavily. He squinted as salt water dripped into his eyes. Nearly out of breath he quietly spoke, "I saw her fall, and I raced to help her."

Lizzy had just made her way down from the cliff. She had pulled up her dress slightly and sprinted to the beach. She saw the body language of the guards and defended Hideki. "I saw the whole thing. This boy saved Princess Maili!"

The princess started coughing as several village *wahines*; village women, approached to give aid. As the guards stepped back, they looked at Hideki.

Koa, a royal guardsman said, "Do you know what you have done?"

Hideki stood silent, expecting to be punished.

"Princess Maili has been saved! You are a hero, *keiki*! Oooo Cousin', look at those wounds. We better get you cleaned up!"

The guards picked Hideki up gently. The six wahines picked up the princess and began to carry her back to the village.

Hideki looked at Lizzy, "I saw someone in the cave." Lizzy looked at Hideki with disbelief.

Po, hoping to get some recognition, walked over to the guards and said, "Hideki's my best friend." Koa patted his head and said, "Good work Cousin'. Your swift feet brought help."

Chapter 2
The Heroes Meet the Queen
Poipu, Kaua'i, June 16, 1899

Queen Lili'oukalani rode as quickly as she could in her carriage to the town medical center in Poipu. The word of the near death of her beloved niece, Princess Maili, frightened her immensely. Not only was she the only niece of the queen, she was also the heir to the throne of Hawai'i. Not having an heir could motivate the sugar farmers to attempt another coup d'etat.

Queen Lydia is what many close to the *mōʻī*, monarch, called her, rode all the way from Princeville; a long day's ride. The constant showers of the east coast of Kaua'i made all of the roads muddy and difficult to pass. A long day's boat ride was also an option, but the queen dreaded seasickness more than the jolting of a four-hour carriage ride.

The word spread that Queen Lydia was on her way. She arrived in the late afternoon. With an explosion of heat, as if the gods knew of her arrival, the sun burst through the clouds. The streets were lined with admirers. This gave Queen Lydia great joy. Kaua'i was the last of the islands to show support for her majesty. However, her connection with the *wahines* was improving all over the islands. The queen always strove to help women's causes.

Koa opened the carriage door, and escorted Lydia inside. The hospital was one of Queen Lydia's projects. She looked around with pride to see the tremendous health care being given to the islanders. The building was bright, white, and clean.

A hospital administrator met the queen at the doorway, and bowed and said, "Aloha and *e 'olu'olu e komo mai*", (please come in). Queen Lydia smiled and bowed in return and said, "Aloha."

This was the queen's first visit to the facility. Lydia chatted politely with the administrator as she was escorted into Princess Maili's room.

As the door to Maili's room opened, the queen could see Maili's sweet smile. Both she and the queen broke out in tears of joy.

"Aloha, my love. How are you feeling?" The queen leaned in and hugged her niece.

Princess Maili shimmied up the bed a bit to sit up tall, "Oh Auntie, I mean, Your Majesty, I feel just fine. Mostly embarrassed."

The queen looked to the corner of the room and saw Maili's friend Lizzy Doel and two young boys. She looked at them for a moment and smiled.

"Miss Lizzy, I understand you were with Princess Maili?"

Lizzy curtsied and looked down in shame, "I can't apologize enough for not taking better care of the princess, Your Majesty."

"Miss Lizzy, you are her friend, not her bodyguard. I think we all know who is to blame for the situation." The queen slowly looked back at the princess as Maili slowly covered her face with her sheets.

"I dare to think what Maili's father is going to say when he gets word." She continued to glare at the princess.

She turned back to the boys in the room, "Who might you young men be?"

Awkwardly the boys curtsied, and the girls giggled. "I am Hideki Yamamoto."

"I am Po San."

"So, you are the two I need to thank for saving my dear niece?" She walked over to Hideki, "May I see your arm?"

Hideki stuck out his injured arm, "My, you did risk your life?"

Po San pointed at Hideki, "I just ran to get help. Hideki is the big hero."

The queen continued to stare at the boys, "Well getting the adults to help was very brave too, Po. Thank you Hideki for swimming in that rough surf. Po San is right. You are a hero. You saved the life of the heir to the throne of Hawai'i. I promise you will be rewarded."

The queen turned back to Lizzy and Maili, "Now, tell me please why you were on those dangerous cliffs!"

Maili lowered the sheets onto her lap, took a breath, and explained, "Auntie Lydia, we have heard so much about the Menehune from so many people. I wanted to see their cave for myself. I mean, if I am going to be queen one day, I will rule over all Hawaiians right? Aren't Menehune the original Hawaiians?"

"Didn't I JUST warn you about that cave?" Lydia glared at Maili, "It is called The Forbidden Cave for a reason, Princess. 'If', the Menehune do exist, then yes. King David and Koa both swore they existed." Lydia squinted to show she was serious. "Lizzy, is this true?"

"Yes, Your Majesty. All the people here swear they are only three to four feet tall, they work at night, and live in caves and in the jungles up in the mountains." Lizzy was showing her excitement.

"In all honesty Princess, when the Merrie Monarch first told me about the Menehune, I was curious too. However, not so curious I'd risk my life, AND my best friend's life." Once again she squinted her eyes to show her displeasure. "I hope you have learned your lesson. Please let the anthropologists do the exploring from now on! Pinkie-swear?"

"Yes Your Majesty, I pinky-swear." The queen and princess hooked their pinkies.

A nurse entered the room and curtsied. Lydia stepped back out of the nurse's way, "So let me hear it from you Maili. What really happened?"

Maili cleared her throat, "Well Auntie, we were tiptoeing out on the point at Shipwreck Beach. It was pretty windy, which made it scary. I got as far as I could to look back into the Menehune Cave, and I remember looking at Lizzy… and then BOOM! I think I belly flopped into the ocean! Next thing I know I am in this bed."

Lizzy stepped forward, "Your Majesty, she is telling the truth. The earth just cracked and she fell straight down. Luckily she missed the rocks. Then I crawled to the edge and I saw Hideki fighting the swells and dragged the princess back to the beach."

Hideki curtsied. The girls giggled again. He looked confused.

Lizzy said, "Boys bow, and girls curtsy."

Hideki turned and punched Po San in the arm, "I told you, stupid."

"Your Majesty, Po San and I were fishing. We saw the two girls up there. Suddenly she fell straight down into the surf. I told Po to run and get help because he's a fast runner. I knew I had to try to help, and luckily she didn't hit any rocks."

There was a knock on the door. Po San's father came in and took a knee while looking at the floor. His clothes were black, torn, and dusty. "Please forgive me, Your Majesty for interrupting, but I must take Po San back to O'ahu immediately! I just found out that his older sister, Jo, is being shipped to Moloka'i in two days." His voice cracked with sorrow.

Po San asked, "Why does she have to go to Moloka'i, Father?" Ho could not answer. Po's father had too many feelings and thoughts twirling in his head. Speaking might reveal how emotional he really was, and Ho did not want to cry in front of his son.

The queen bowed her head, "I am sorry Po San, but that's where they take the lepers. Unfortunately she will have to live there for the rest of her life."

Po San failed to understand, "Father, is this true?"

Ho shook his head yes.

"But why?" Po San raised his voice.

The queen walked towards the young boy and placed her hand on his shoulder. "Po San, leprosy is a very contagious and deadly disease. If we do not isolate the people who have it, we will all get it eventually. You wouldn't want that would you?"

"But you are the queen. Can't you make her stay?"

"My dear boy, it is under my direct order that we do this to protect all the Hawaiian people, especially the uninfected."

Po San ran out of the hospital room.

The queen walked over to Po's father Ho, "Please Mr. San, please join me on the queen's ship. We will leave immediately. My ship can get us back to O'ahu and to your daughter by tomorrow morning."

Ho tried to compose himself, "Thank you for your generosity, Your Majesty. How can I repay you?"

"There is no need. Po San saved the princess. It's the least I can do. And you, and you, and you," pointing at the children, "are all coming along."

Hideki bowed again awkwardly, "Your Majesty, I have to get my father's permission."

"KOA!" The queen summoned her guardsman, "Tell our captain we leave as soon as possible. Then take Hideki to his father and tell him of the queen's requests. Hideki is going to have a little summer vacation at the queen's palace. He might want to bring some more clothes."

Koa nodded and gave the queen a smile before he left to carry out her orders.

Chapter 3
Jo & Moloka'i
Pearl Harbor, June 17, 1899

The clouds in the morning off the coast of Pearl Harbor are often a collection of purple, gray, and white as they float across the Pacific sky. The sun had risen just above the horizon. Off in the distance was the queen's ship. It was steaming at full speed with thick, black smoke from the coal engine spewing into the turquoise sky as it approached Pearl Harbor.

After the Reciprocity Act of 1874, the United States and the Kingdom of Hawai'i made an agreement for the U.S. Navy to anchor their ships in the bay. In exchange, Hawai'i paid no import taxes on the sugar imported to America. As much as King David had disliked America slowly influencing his kingdom, the technology, the supplies, and the dredging of the harbor created revenue for the islands. Ships from around the world would stop in Hawai'i for an opportunity to get fresh supplies, the crew to enjoy a nice meal, as well as take in the beautiful scenery. They spent money, which helped the Hawaiian economy. This made all of the shopkeepers and restaurant owners very happy. Kicking out the Americans and

others would have had a devastating impact on the Hawaiian businesses. Now ten years into her reign, Queen Lydia would encourage trade, but it came at a cost.

Queen Lydia and Maili were about to have their first grown up conversation. The two royal travelers were on deck as they approached Pearl Harbor.

Maili leaned on her auntie, "Auntie Lydia, O'ahu sure is beautiful." The little royal family was enjoying the swaying palm trees, the white caps of the waves breaking on shore, and the green mountains as they rose into the clouds.

Lydia wrapped her shawl around her, "Yes it is my dear."

"Look! Auntie a rainbow!" Maili said as she bounced on her toes. The rainbow started at Diamond Head and crossed into Manoa Valley. Suddenly Maili's mood changed as a thought entered her head, "Auntie, why do people get leprosy? I am sad for Po's sister, and their family. I don't have a sister, but I bet it would be sad to lose one."

"Princess, I do not know, but I have seen what it can do. It is a horrible disease. It does not

kill you quickly. It slowly eats away at all of your skin until ..." the cool Pacific air gave Lydia a chill, and she brought Maili in closer.

"Until what Auntie?" Maili looked up at the queen with wonderment.

"Well my dear, until it kills you. There is no cure, so as painful as separating families is, imagine how painful it would be if leprosy spread to everyone? Sometimes I wonder if opening up Pearl Harbor to the world was a good thing for Hawai'i."

As the world became aware of Hawai'i, thousands of immigrants came to the islands. These immigrants became the new workforce and backbone of the new economy. Ironically, many of them brought disease that would decimate the native Hawaiian population. The Hawaiian traditions were being chipped away. Because of this, some wanted to overthrow the monarchy.

"Auntie?" Maili stared at the buildings of Honolulu. "Would you send me to Moloka'i if I got leprosy?"

"Let's not think of such unpleasant thoughts My Princess. Treat lepers with dignity, but do not get too close to them, EVER! Lydia looked

down on the little princess. "Our doctors still don't know how contagious it is."

Maili had fear in her eyes, "What does 'contagious' mean?"

"How easily it spreads from person to person. Unfortunately, it impacted the Chinese community the worst when they started arriving in the 1850's. Many of the Hawaiians even call leprosy *Ma-i-Pake*: the Chinese disease."

June 15, 1899 – two days prior

Jo was playing at school when Mrs. Appleton called her over. "Jo, I see you have a sore on your thigh. How long have you had that?"

Jo looked down, "Oh I cut myself while doing chores the other day," Jo lied. Jo had noticed the sore several weeks before. She had forgotten about it when she wore shorts that day.

"Hmmm. Ok, thank you." Mrs. Appleton turned and walked away. Jo continued to play hopscotch, thinking her lie had worked.

Just as school was about to get out, a young man the children had never seen before came to the classroom door. Mrs. Appleton walked over and stepped outside for a moment. The children started to wonder if someone was in trouble. When Mrs. Appleton returned, she looked at Jo and asked her to step outside. Jo knew what this meant. She had heard the conversation about leprosy and how it was spreading through the community. Jo was so nervous she almost threw up. She started to cry as all the children looked at her with suspicion. Some mean girls leaned towards each other and whispered. They too knew what was about to happen. This was not the first time a child in their school was taken away. Jo walked outside and the man escorted her to the nurse's office.

The man was from the Hawaiian Department of Health. Principal Wehr stepped in to observe. "Please sit down Jo. I understand you have a sore on your leg. Would you mind lifting up your shorts a bit?"

Jo was shaking with fear; tears were rolling down her face as she sniffed.

Principal Wehr said, "It's ok my dear. Do as he says."

The man said, "Please keep looking out the window. This should not hurt a bit." The man took out a two-inch needle and proceeded to insert it almost entirely into the wound. Jo peaked through the corner of her eyes, and to her amazement, she felt no pain. The man looked at the principal and shook his head, which affirmed his suspicion. Principal Wehr looked to the ground with deep sadness. Leprosy deadened all the nerves around the open wound and it was a sure sign Jo was positive.

"I'm afraid I need to take you home dear. I need to talk to your parents." The stranger said.

They drove a mile or so up a red dusty road to the San residence. The San's had moved from Haleiwa, just months after they landed in Hawai'i. The tiny house was made in haste, but had held together after several storms, constant rain, and trade winds.

Jo's mom Su saw the car coming up the road and walked out of the front door letting the screen door slam behind her. She had to wipe her hands on a towel from the sticky rice on her fingertips. She stopped a few feet into her yard. She again used the towel on her shoulder to wipe the sweat off of her forehead. A tall white man in a dark suit she'd never seen before got out of the car. It was the first time Su had ever seen a car. Jo climbed out of the passenger seat. Su knew something was wrong, very wrong!

Jo ran into Su's arms and cried uncontrollably. "May I help you sir?" Su asked.

The man took off his hat as a sign of respect and proceeded to tell Su Jo's medical condition. "So as I am sure you are well aware, Jo must come with me immediately to the Quarantine Center. In a few days the next ship is expected to depart. She will be sent to the leper colony at Kalaupapa on Moloka'i for the remainder of her life," he said sadly. "I suggest you inform any relative who wants to say farewell to come to the Quarantine Center as soon as possible. I can give you a few minutes to gather her things."

Su and Jo hugged and cried.

After the most painful conversation Jo's mother had ever had, the man from the Department of Health allowed Jo to fill up a small suitcase, and then he drove her to the Quarantine Center in Honolulu. There she would wait for the ship to Moloka'i, which had arrived the night before, and was set to leave at noon.

Queen Lydia used thousands of dollars of resources to ensure the lepers had what they needed. The lepers also received assistance from family members who sent care packages and letters to their relatives. Po and his father were given an hour to visit with Jo before she had to leave. Queen Lydia gave her personal carriage to the Sans to get them to the Quarantine Center in time to say their farewell to Jo.

The Quarantine Center in Honolulu had a double fence. Families were not allowed to touch, hug, kiss, or have any contact with the infected. Jo ran to the fence when she saw her family. She screamed, "Father, please don't let them take me away!"

Ho collapsed to his knees and wept. Po grabbed the fence as if to climb it, but he knew it would do no good. Even at his young age he realized that this was the last time he'd probably ever see his sister and wanted to cheer her up. "Sister, I hear they have good schools on Moloka'i, and they have really good food. The queen told me so. Several cooks are there now and they cook great meals."

Her voice trailed off, "I don't care about food." The family just remained silent for the next few minutes until the guard came by and said, "It is time."

Po and his father waved sadly as Jo was escorted away. Jo kept looking back for one last glimpse. She used to love Honolulu, but now found herself hating everything about the city. Jo went through the metal door. The family would likely never see Jo again. Even though it was legal to travel to Moloka'i, Hawaiians could not land on the leper colony. They could take a dinghy to the pier and talk for a few minutes as suppliers loaded the docks with food, medical supplies, and clothing donated by the empathetic in O'ahu. This however cost money, of which Ho and his wife Su had little to none.

The father and son took the queen's carriage back to Iolani Palace. Po was to meet up with Hideki, and Ho wanted to thank the queen for the carriage ride.

Queen Lydia and the children walked to the steps of the palace to greet the Sans. "Thank you, Your Highness. It was because of you I got to see my daughter one last time," Ho said sadly as he looked at the ground.

Po shouted, "Because of you my sister is gone forever!"

Hideki slapped Po across the face, "Don't you ever talk like that to the queen again!"

Queen Lydia walked over to Po, "I can't express in words how sorry I am Po, but remember, if Jo isn't removed from here, then maybe your mother and father may catch leprosy and they too would have to go. You wouldn't want that would you?"

Po cried for a moment and then responded, "No."

Ho hugged his son, "I must go now. Your mother needs me. The walk is long. Farewell my son." Ho felt conflicted about leaving his son. Both of his children were now gone. He hoped the slap Hideki gave him was out of character.

Ho turned and began the five-mile walk to his home. Hideki walked over and put his arm around Po, "Now listen Po, I didn't want to slap you, but you can't talk to the queen like that ever again, ok?"

The four children walked inside together for dinner. It was June in O'ahu. The four friends would begin a long time friendship that summer of 1899.

Later that afternoon

A few hours later as the sun was dipping behind the steep mountain cliffs of Moloka'i, Jo was lowered onto a dinghy loaded with supplies. A couple men began rowing towards the pier. The waves were quite high and Jo was very scared. She wasn't a strong swimmer. When they reached the pier, Jo climbed up a small ladder and looked at all the people who were there to greet her. Some of the men started assembling a pulley system to raise the supplies onto the dock. The lepers of

Moloka'i looked to the supply ship as the most interesting part of the week. Would new people be arriving? Would some of them get mail? Were new fashions or technology brought onto the island?

Beyond the dock was the quaint little village of Kalaupapa: shops, restaurants, and many friendly people. Some villagers looked as normal as people did in Honolulu. It was hard to imagine why they were even there. However, some had a severe condition on their faces; those wore a hood to protect newcomers from the shock. Jo tried not to stare, but their faces looked as if they were made of wax and had partially melted. Other people smiled at her hoping to ease the pain of her transition.

As she walked down the splintered slats of the pier, a priest approached her, "You must be Jo?"

"Yes I am. What happens to me now?" Jo asked the priest.

"I'm Father Roger. I took over after Father Damien passed away. I'm sure you have heard of him?" Jo shook her head yes. "Let me carry your suitcase. You are very lucky Jo. You will be fostered by 'Sister Dorothy'. She specifically prayed for your safe arrival. She is currently preparing supper for you. She will be your foster mother. Dorothy has been here for some time and will give you all the rules and expectations. Everyone is expected to contribute to the survival of Kalaupapa. As a child, you are expected to go to school, and go to church on Sundays. That's pretty much it."

Jo looked up at Father Roger and cracked a half smile, "That doesn't sound so bad. Are there many children here?"

"Unfortunately my little sister, there are quite a few. They will help you get assimilated into our world. It is different, yet the same." Jo stopped for a moment and looked around. Kalapapau was mostly just a small main street with a few businesses. Jo could see small little homes tucked away in the jungle just a few yards away. Her eyes began to water with a cool breeze as it came off the mountain and struck her face. The mountain appeared to be thousands of feet straight up. It was already hiding in its own shadow and the detail was difficult to make out. However the filtered sunlight was still bright enough to heighten all the reds, yellows and oranges of the tropical flowers that sprinkled throughout the neighbors' gardens.

The two arrived at Sister Dorothy's house, and Father Roger knocked. "One minute!" a voice could be heard through the door. A moment later the door opened. Sister Dorothy stood inside the doorway, all five feet and 95 pounds of her. She was wearing monk's clothes and looked healthy. She was part Chinese and part Hawaiian. "She is rather pretty for someone so old," Jo thought.

Dorothy was 35 and had been on the island for 15 years.

Dorothy slowly shuffled backwards as she opened the door wide enough for Jo to walk in. "I will see you at church Sunday, yes?" asked Father Roger.

"Have I ever missed a sermon?" Dorothy replied.

Father Roger thought for a second, "There was that one time during the hurricane." Dorothy looked at him with a silly grin, "Aloha Father," and she closed the door.

Sister Dorothy shuffled slowly as she closed the door. "Please drop your suitcase and have a seat my dear. Supper is almost ready. I have so many questions for you. You aren't shy are you?"

"No ma'am. I am rather hungry though. They did not feed me on the boat. In fact, they barely looked at me."

Dorothy sat down in her favorite chair and exposed her mangled feet. Jo accidentally gasped! "Oh my feet? Yes, that is where I am afflicted. Leprosy is a strange disease. If I had no feet, you couldn't tell I was a leper at all. Some poor souls only have sores on their faces. They can run like the wind, but are hideous to look at. I would love to run again, but love my face more." Dorothy laughed at her own joke. "Just to let you know, I move slowly because I cannot feel anything with my feet. My legs are strong, but it's like walking on pillows. I am quite unstable really. Now that you're here, the one favor I would ask is for you to inspect my feet. I know it is grotesque; but if I cut my foot, I'd never know, and an infection would kill me. That's how most of us die, a simple wound in our infected area. It festers and slowly kills us. Where is your infection Jo?"

I have just a little patch on my thigh. I watched the doctor put a needle deep inside of it and I couldn't feel anything."

"That's how it is with my feet. That actually is a good place to have it. Your pretty face remains, and you can still run. Well enough about that horrible disease. Let me get supper ready. I made some fish stew: fresh catch of the day and some vegetables. We actually eat quite well here."

"That's the last thing my brother Po said to me."

"Well Po was right. Most of us have gardens. We have all the fish and crab you could ever want. The weekly supply ship drops off seasonings, and families donate other food. In town we can buy or trade for beef. There are plenty of shops on Main Street where you can get chickens and eggs as well."

"People have money here?" Jo questioned.

"Oh sure. It's just like Honolulu, except you can't leave. There are hospitals, churches, schools, banks, restaurants, and boutiques. We even have a community center where we have celebrations. We try to keep life as normal as possible. And you get used to people looking different and walking funny."

"Oh that's really neat. What about the children at school? When do I start?"

"Well lucky for you it's summer vacation, just like O'ahu schools. You will see the children playing tomorrow. Most know you arrived. Some might come by to say 'Aloha'. Oh, before I forget. We have a strict curfew here. One hour after dark, the town square bell will ring three times. Everyone has ten minutes to get home. All the shops and restaurants close well before the bells. And if you were wondering, yes we have a sheriff and a jail in the colony. So please don't sneak out."

"Oh my, I'd never do that!" Jo said.

"Ha! That's what they all say. Kids get bored. They sneak out all of the time. They get caught and their foster parents have to bail them out. I hope you won't ever do that."

"No Ma'am; I promise."

"Great. Now all that is settled, let's eat!"

Chapter 4

Three of the Thirteen
Haleiwa, West Side of O'ahu, September 10,
1887

Several years prior …

"O'ahu is such a beautiful island." Sanford
Dole thought to himself as he slowly rode his
horse to visit an unhappy farmer. He was
riding alongside Walter Blake. Walter was
from California and represented several
California sugar farmers. He had just
graduated with a business degree from
Stanford. For Walter only being 21, Dole was
impressed with Walter's quick understanding
of the sugarcane industry in O'ahu.

Walter remarked, "This island is simply
beautiful Mr. Dole! I never knew there were so
many shades of green!" Walter sniffed deeply,
"Oh my, I can smell pineapples. Why do sugar
and pineapple grow so well here?"

"That's a great question Walter. If you look
over there, and over there, both Ko'olau and
Wainanae Mountain ranges run North West
separated by only ten miles. The way they are
directed, they tend to block all major storms.
This reduces the soil runoff."

"What makes the soil so good?" Walter wondered out loud.

"Oh, it's the volcanoes. In the northwest region of O'ahu, the towns of Waialua and Haleiwa became prosperous farming towns because they are right here in the middle of these fertile fields."

Dole pointed out to the horizon, "We also envision tourists staying here one day. The views are majestic. Just look at these green fields and those shear-jagged mountains are like nothing I've ever seen. An elevated and clear view from a resident's second floor, they could easily see south/southeast for miles; such a rich and lush valley."

"Mr. Dole, I can envision a tall hotel right over there. While standing on their balcony, people will notice the red-orange dirt that contrasts with the vibrant dark green vegetation that continues onto the horizon and eventually covers most of the mountains! What a gorgeous view! More and more these days wealthy Americans are looking for new and exciting ways to travel. Plus there is a growing middle class with a desire to travel."

"Look at how the different shades of green vegetation go up on some mountains to their peaks. The valley slowly slopes towards the Koʻolau Mountains to the north. From this vantage point looking northwest, the mighty, crystal blue Pacific crashes onto Oʻahu's beaches. You are right Mr. Blake, gorgeous!"

While sitting high in their saddles, Sanford and Walter could see thousands of acres of sugarcane and pineapple fields. These nearly went to the horizon. What disturbed Sanford was what he did not see. He found himself disgruntled in the midst of all of this beauty.

Blake stopped and stared at the beautiful landscape, "So how did all of this begin? I mean who thought of sugarcane and pineapple?"

"As the missionaries started arriving in the early 1800's, they soon discovered the rich, ancient volcanic soil was ideal for growing sugarcane and later pineapples from Central America. Eventually, farmers would experiment with coffee on other islands. At the proper elevations, around 2,000-4,000 feet, Kona and Kauaʻi coffees have become some of the finest coffees in the world. Those coffees are grown on those islands."

"That is interesting; similar to South America." Walter quipped, trying to impress Mr. Dole with his knowledge.

"Farming was prosperous for nearly all who ventured here. As the word spread, farmers from Japan, China, America, and Portugal flocked to the island. American ingenuity, technology, and a strong work ethic created a lot of wealth for not just the farmers, but this entire region. We pay our fair share of taxes to make the king wealthier too. Unfortunately labor issues are a constant problem in the Hawaiian Islands, which are often created by the king. To make things worse, the Hawaiians are dropping like flies. Since the 1800's when the natives became exposed to smallpox, measles, and later leprosy, they have died by the thousands! Tragic really."

"Oh my. That's horrible!" Walter pulled the reins of his horse as he struggled to keep his horse on the path.

"Well despite these struggles, farmers fight the daily battles of irrigation, labor, pests, thieves, and politics. The potential to make great amounts of money lured many Americans to Hawai'i. However, the stresses of keeping their farms profitable are weighing heavily on the *haoles*; that's what the Hawaiians call us."

Sanford and Walter got off their horses. The ride had been ten miles from his farm. He led his horse, Whinny, by the reins. They walked over to a hitching post and tied up their horses. The puffy white clouds moved quickly over the sky. The sun seemed to explode from behind the clouds, and the light stung for a second when it hit Sanford's skin. He stroked Whinny's face a few times, and she started to drink from the trough.

Walter looked up at the sky, "Man the sun sure gets hot here!"

Rubert Anderson walked out of his the screen door, "Good afternoon Mr. Dole. How was the ride?" He continued down the steps to shake his hand.

"Oh Whinny always gives me a smooth ride. This is Walter Blake. He's a businessman from California and wants to help improve demand for sugar there."

"Pleased to meet you Mr. Blake." The two shook hands. "We could definitely use some help these days."

Dole looked around at the acres of sugarcane still in the ground. Only a few men were working in the adjacent fields. "You look like you're in trouble, Rubert."

"Volney Ashford and I have had to share crews. Our last Japanese crew just walked off. They said King David called them to head out to some southern fields that he profits from. He's killing us!" They heard the clip clop of a horse. They could see the top of a cowboy hat as it slowly bounced up and down through the taller sugarcanes. Rubert's neighbor came into view. "Here comes Volney right now. He can tell you."

Volney Ashford owned 100 acres of sugar and pineapple fields south of Haleiwa. He was a large man and quite popular among *The Riflemen*. These were men who compared themselves to *the Minutemen* of Lexington and Concord. Volney got off his horse. Rubert walked over to him. They slapped each other on the backs. Rubert was a large man, standing at 6'2" and Volney was clearly taller. "How are the crews working out Volney?"

Volney took off his cowboy hat and dusted off his Levis with it, "Luckily this crew has made great progress with my sugarcane, but now my pineapples are about to go bad. Thank God these Portuguese are hard workers. The crew of Japanese workers that King David took from us really set us back, Mr. Dole. Is there anything you can do?"

Sanford took off his hat and patted his revolver on his side, "The *Committee of Thirteen* wants to pay a visit to the king, and I think having *the Riflemen* backing us up will send a clear message."

Sanford looked at Walter, "What are your thoughts son?"

Walter interrupted, "Please forgive me gentlemen, but may I suggest we use technology to help reduce the need for labor. There are several new devices that American farmers are using that work like one hundred men. They are expensive, but will save you money in the long run. You won't have to rely on labor as much after you buy a couple of the newest machines. I realize this is a long-term solution. However, for the short term, I would give bonuses when fields are done. Give them incentives to stay with you."

Volney asked, "And who might you be, Sir?"

Sanford said, "Please forgive my manners. This is Walter Blake from California. He has a business degree from Stanford and is here to help the American farmers."

Volney tightened the cinch under the horse, "Well Mr. Dole, and Mr. Blake, all of the farmers around here are having issues. Just recently some savages from Makaha snuck onto our farms in the middle of the night and stole hundreds of pineapples. I don't know how they did it. There was a half moon, but that's not a lot of light. A farm hand up early scared them off. They started running west after he fired a shot."

Dole raised his voice, clearly irritated, "We will have to bring this up with the king, but until then, perhaps we should have a posse ride over there and scare the hell out of them. I would also set up nightly security teams. The villagers from Makaha are known to be quite aggressive. Always have more than one armed man out at night."

Rubert's wife, Tracy, approached from the house, "Would any of you gentlemen care for some tea? I have some fresh baked cookies as well." Tracy was half Hawaiian and half American. She was born in Honolulu and had lived her entire life on O'ahu. She was tall and tan. Her modest dress could not hide her figure. Being well endowed made her a favorite of most of the workers. Some would say they would rather work for Miss Tracy than any other woman on the island. Her father was one of the early missionaries and her mother was a local. Tracy was never a fan of the Hawaiian kings after she learned of the atrocities committed by King Kamehameha's soldiers on her elders.

Volney and Sanford said, "Yes, ma'am." in unison.

The men ate a few cookies and sipped some tea as they plotted their next move.

"So it's settled. Volney, you rally your *Riflemen* and be ready on October 3 in Honolulu. Rubert, you are going to round up extra ammunition and rifles. Let's make sure every man is well prepared."

Disturbed by the planning of violence, Walter decided to head back to San Francisco. However, before he departed, he arranged a clandestine meeting in Honolulu.

The men shook hands and rode back to their fields. In the next few days Sanford Dole rode to two other farms to increase his numbers. It appeared the time had come for the American businessmen to confront the king.

Waipahu, a few miles west of Honolulu

Not far away was the American attorney, Lorrin Thurston. He had arrived just a few hours prior from Pearl Harbor. A special delivery had been shipped from San Francisco: copies of the British and American constitutions. He had been instructed by Sanford Dole to write a constitution to be used for Hawai'i after *The Hawaiian League* would take power from King Kalakaua.

The new government would be called a "Constitutional Monarchy". This way, the revolutionaries could claim the king still had power. This would prevent the Hawaiians from revolting and any other country from intervening. The truth was the revolutionaries were going to control the legislature and increase their own power.

Lorrin walked up to his midtown office and unlocked his front door. The streets were busy with shoppers and passers by. He could hear the clomping of boots on the slats of wood that raised the sidewalks out of the often-muddy road. He looked left and right more than once. Those sounds made him nervous. Lorrin had multiple locks on his front door. Security was crucial having so many of his clients' confidential records inside. Now he would have the seeds of a revolution to add to his documents. He walked into the lobby and relocked two more locks from the inside.

"Steven!" Lorrin yelled. " I'm back and I need your assistance."

Steven Schadefbal had been napping. It was time to get to work. Lorrin was always tickled with Steven's whiskers, which grew randomly around his face. These coarse black whiskers protruded from his nose, eyebrows, and ears. Lorrin found Steven's facial hair to be quite odd. "Coming Mr. Thurston." Steven threw on his jacket and lumbered down the stairs. "Did they arrive?"

"Yes Steven; both of them. We need to get to work. I figure these two documents are probably the best-written political documents in the history of the world. The British and the Americans have already done most of the work for us. We just need to use their words to fit our needs."

Steven opened up the blinds to brighten the room with the afternoon sunshine. He was often bothered with the way sunlight lit the room brilliantly for several moments, and then as the trade winds did most days, pushed a thick cloud that would float over the office. It was like a switch would turn off 80% of the light instantly.

Steven asked, "Have you thought of a preamble?"

"I have Steven. I think it'll go something like this."

We the citizens of Hawai'i, in order to form a better democracy, while establishing justice, ensuring domestic tranquility among all the Hawaiian Islands, providing for the general welfare of the king's citizens, and having the right to provide for the common defense for ourselves and all future Hawaiian citizens, do ordain and establish this Constitutional Monarchy for the Republic of Hawai'i.

"Wow Mr. Thurston, that is impressive. But I have some questions." Steven said.

"Of course, my good Lad."

"We are the minority here. Won't all the islanders out vote us?"

"That is a great question. We will make it law that only landowners can vote. We do not want everyone to vote. That wouldn't make any sense. The problem with democracies is that once the common man realizes he can vote, the have-nots will never stop voting and take away from those who have. So eventually all democracies fail. However, our plan will drastically limit all of their numbers, and use their own traditions against them. You see Steven, they don't allow women to own land. They pass it down to the next male heir. So women will never be able to vote. Moreover my good man, I am sure the legislature will prevent easy access for Hawaiians to purchase new lands, preserving our power for generations!"

"That's brilliant Mr. Thurston!"

"The Chinese and Japanese workers don't have a democratic tradition, and the Portuguese are new here. I figure after forcing the king to sign this, we will have a peaceful transition of power. Then my clients' profits will sky rocket once again."

"What if the king resists?"

Lorrin looked at Steven. He looked out the window. He looked back at Steven again. "I have no personal ill will against the king, and I don't want to imagine what could happen to him." He looked back at the documents with no emotions in his eyes.

Chapter 5
The Merrie Monarch
Honolulu, The Imperial Palace, Oct. 3, 1887

King David La'amea Kalākaua had ruled Hawai'i for just a few years. He was known as the Merrie Monarch due to his love to celebrate, dance, and sing. He reinstituted old Hawaiian traditions like the hula, the luau, and reinforced that written Hawaiian language be taught in schools.

However, in his short rule, King Kalākaua, or King David, had made many political enemies and felt the need to protect the throne. It was time to name an heir apparent. King David summoned Princess Lydia, his sister, to his private meeting chambers.

The princess was born on September 2, 1838 with the given name Lydia Liliʻu Loloku Walania Wewehi Kamaka'eha. David had four other siblings, but he always trusted Lydia the most. She had become quite popular among the islanders, especially women. Lydia worked much of her adult life promoting women's rights on the islands. Lydia would often say her proudest moment was the opening of the Queen's Hospital in 1860. Lydia literally went door to door to raise finances for the hospital. The native population had been decimated by disease brought by foreigners. Estimates of nearly 85% of native Hawaiians died in the 1800's due to disease. With the Chinese immigrants in the 1850's came leprosy. This affliction spread throughout the islands and a leper colony was created in Kalaupapa on the remote northern peninsula of Moloka'i. There was a great need for health care on the islands, and Princess Lydia had made this her priority.

In Honolulu, in Iolani, (i oh lah nee) Palace the king's doors were grand and ornate. The entrance to the king's chamber was protected by two royal guards. They were dressed much like most guards of modern day Europe, which was definitely not comfortable attire for 85 degrees and 80 % humidity.

Princess Lydia Lili'oukalani approached the door as her formal gown dragged the hardwood floors. Lydia would only dress this way during official royal business. Western clothes were very heavy and warm. Lydia approached the door but kept her eyes on Koa. She smiled and stopped for a moment, Koa smiled back as he stood tall. Koa opened the door and King David stood at attention.

In a bellowing voice King David cheerfully shouted, "Aloooooo HA Princess!" Lydia curtsied, and in her sweet and soft voice replied, "Aloha, Your Majesty."

King David waved away the guards and said quietly, "Please come in. Get comfortable,

Sister." King David Kalākaua wore his traditional royal coat and sash. He was adorned with several medals. His collar was buttoned and adorned with gold. He was dressed very much like European royalty. He had a dark tan and muscular build. At 5'7", he was shorter than many Americans, yet still looked quite impressive. His popular muttonchops allowed him to fit right into the facial hair fashions of the time period.

Lydia adjusted her dress as she sat down, "Brother, I HATE these dresses. They smell like wet sheep. They are hotter than Pele's temper, and make me feel like I am ten feet under water!"

"Oh sister, as much as I adore you, your fashion issues are the least of our problems." King David looked around once again to see if any of the help had snuck back into his chamber. He lowered his voice, "Listen dear Sister, we have much to discuss in the next few days. After much reflection, I have decided it is time to publicly make you the heir apparent to the throne."

Lydia covered her mouth and was about to cry. "Brother are you well?"

"Oh Lydia you misunderstand. Let me clear up some matters. I am very healthy and have never been happier with the progress we've made in my three years." Lydia's feelings began to calm. "However, politics is a nasty business and I have learned so much about ruling and leadership in these past months. I feel compelled to share my dreams and nightmares with you," David whispered.

"David what is going on?" Lydia asked in a louder voice.

"Shhhh Sister. There are spies everywhere. I am finding it more difficult to trust ANYONE but you. Ever since I was appointed by the legislature, Queen Emma's supporters have been working to undermine me."

Lydia put up her finger to shush David and whispered back, "Why would Hawaiians try to overthrow Hawai'i?"

"You have much to learn, Sister. Power, or the lack of it, stirs the most evil thoughts of mankind. Queen Emma believed she was the rightful ruler of Hawai'i after King Kamehameha IV died. Plus she did get more votes than I did. However, the constitution says the legislature chooses if no direct heir is available. I believe her supporters are still bitter." David continued to pace around the room, "I am conflicted, Sister, between the need to embrace technology and our desires to hold on to the traditional ways. As for Emma, I am not sure where she stands. I know she does respect you. Now we have all these businessmen trying to influence my court and the legislature. I want to share some of the lessons I've learned. So if something happens to me, you can continue our dreams of bringing back all of our traditions to the Hawaiian people."

Lydia appeared puzzled and leaned back in her chair. "You surprised me, Brother. Do you not want progress? Wasn't it you who decreed these western clothes, western technologies, and western business methods?"

The king seemed agitated and began to pace, "Sister, of course I want to modernize. But we can't let others replace our traditions either. We are caught between holding on to our traditions and modernizing."

King David paced around the room some more, "We need trains and ships to help the farmers. If I make a decision without the legislature, they become angry. If I help the pineapple farmers by moving crews, the sugar farmers in Haleiwa will complain. If I help Maui, Kaua'i complains. And Queen Emma's supporters complain about everything! Mauna Loa has continued to flow, cutting the Big Island in half. It's exhausting. But if I don't step up, the legislature and businessmen will take too much power!"

Princess Lydia sat and thought quietly.

David stepped in close to his sister, "What are you thinking about Sister?"

"So many things, Your Majesty. For starters, why you chose me, and not Anna, James, Likelike, or Kuhio. I also think we need to study how the Kamehamehas before us, and other leaders held onto power!" Lydia's head was filled with so many thoughts.

"We can get to that later, Sister. First, I want you to meet the men I chose as your security team. Gentlemen, please come in!" David shouted.

Through the doors walked four of the palace's guards. Lydia was familiar with a few of the men from previous details. "Here are Koa, Tafa, Sione, and Tavita. They will be your around the clock security detail from here on out. At least one of them will be on duty at all times."

Lydia stood and smiled, "Aloha gentlemen." The guards bowed.

The king and princess stopped talking as they heard a strange noise. The royal siblings were distracted by a low rumble. At first they were unsure what it was. It grew louder. It sounded like people yelling. Just then there was a loud knock on the door and it flew open. It was the king's religious advisor, Kenneth Doel.

"Your Majesty! You and the princess must hide! An angry mob is coming this way with guns! I think they mean to harm you!"

King David pounded on his desk, "Where are my guards?"

"Your Majesty, your guards have gone out to slow down the mob, but they have rifles! You must leave NOW for your safety!" Kenneth begged.

King David stared into Princess Lydia's eyes as they began to fill with tears. They both knew this might be the end. "I will address the crowd on the balcony. Koa, I beg of you, protect the princess!"

King David Kalākaua walked upstairs to get to the balcony doors. He pulled them open and walked out onto the balcony. In the royal gardens stood nearly 200 Hawaiians. Most of them were supporters of Queen Emma from the Big Island. Others were villagers from Maui, Kaua'i, and Moloka'i. Many had rifles. Others had signs expressing their complaints. It appeared King David Kalākaua was about to have the shortest reign in Hawaiian history. He raised his hand. He could smell the burning of the oils in the torches as the crowd yelled louder. King David did not notice the princess had followed him and was slightly behind him.

Lydia forced her way through the guards and onto to the balcony.

Softly, the king heard a low, but sweet voice beginning to sing. He walked forward not knowing where it was coming from. Confused, he looked around the balcony. The princess had sung from this spot many times. She knew the power of acoustics. The crowd began to murmur.

"Ha ' aheo ka ua I na pali
the rain is proud on the slopes

Ke nihi a 'ela I ka nahele
When biting the forest

E hahai ana paha I ka liko
It may follow the line

Pua ' ahihi lehua o uka
Upland fire flower

Hui
Hi

Aloha 'oe Aloha 'oe"
I love you, I love you

The rebellious group of armed men and women became silent. Some of the wahines began to sing along. Many of those wahines grabbed their kanes by the arm and sang to them. Most of the anger quickly diminished.

Like a slow moving wave of emotion, a feeling of calm rolled to the back of the crowd. From that moment on, Princess Lydia was the beloved heir apparent to the Hawaiian throne.

Chapter 6
Royal History
The next morning, October 6, 1887,

King David Kalākaua and Princess Lydia
Liliʻoukalani sat quietly at the breakfast
table. All the servants had been asked to
leave, and the siblings were struggling to
gather their thoughts and feelings from the
previous night's events.

Princess Lydia cut through her ham and forked
a piece of pineapple. She chewed a bit and
wiped her mouth, "Your Majesty, I have never
been so afraid for my life as I was last night.
What you did was the most reckless thing you
could have done. If things had turned out
differently, I would be without my brother and
Hawai'i would be without their king."

"Let's please cut with the formalities, Sister. I
felt dealing with them was much smarter than
running away. If we had escaped, we would
still be dealing with this today," King David
replied.

"Well then, Brother, if you hadn't cut me off I
would have also told you I thought that was
the bravest thing you have ever done. I was,
and am, so proud of the Merrie Monarch
today." She said with a smile.

King David sat quietly, and reflected on his sister's compliment, "Well your singing I believe was even more brave. If things had gone south, I would be without a sister and Hawai'i would be without an heir to the throne."

Lydia changed the subject. "Yesterday you were going to tell me about early Hawaiians and their kings. What do you know about such things?" The princess leaned in and listened.

David sipped his tea and cleared his throat, "Our royal historians tell of the legends of the original Hawaiians called the Menehune. They are the little people of the islands. In fact, Kaua'ians claim to see them, and their work, to this day. They are only three feet tall, yet have incredible skills."

"Do you believe these rumors?"

"These rumors, as you say, have been around for hundreds of years. Did our ancestors lie?" David looked over his cup of tea. "Royal historians say that when the original Polynesians arrived, they found no people here. However large fishponds were created out of perfectly cut and stacked lava rocks. Rocks so large, four of our mightiest warriors would have difficulty moving them."

Lydia played with her food for a moment, "Well if that is true, Brother, then I deduce that they weren't the original Hawaiians. The Menehune were!" She raised her eyebrow at the king. "When I become queen, I want ALL Hawaiians to know that I will rule on all of their behalf, from the little Menehune to the lepers in Kalapapau!" Lydia looked David in the eyes, "So what happened to those original Polynesians?"

"Sister, this is where Hawaiian tradition begins. The original Hawaiians sailed from the Marquesas Islands, which is nearly 2,000 miles south. The early Hawaiians lived in peace and moderate prosperity, I'm told, for 800 years. Historians are still digging up older and older artifacts. Many of which they believe, have been claimed by Pele's lava. Unfortunately, the warlike Polynesians showed up about 500 years ago. Through much war and death, they would begin what we now know as Hawaiian culture."

Lydia loosened her collar, which was choking her a bit, "That makes sense. We are a prosperous people still today, but will fight if need be."

"For those 500 years, Sister, we Hawaiians did not live in peace with each other. Our islands were isolated from the rest of the world and we became quite independent. Trade was abundant, but our warring chiefs would slaughter other islanders out of jealousy or spite. It makes no sense to me as they were trade partners. It was a horrible part of our history, dear Sister!" King David appeared to be ashamed.

Lydia replied, "But we are not like that, dear Brother. You are the Merrie Monarch, and you will bring peace and prosperity to all the Hawaiians from every island."

"I feel compelled to share perhaps the worst part of our history. Our people and culture would be changed forever with the arrival of Captain Cook in the late 1700's. After he first visited the Big Island nearly 100 years ago it all quickly changed. Our traditions were tested with the technologies of the west. The people from the Big Island acquired the weapons and foods of the Westerners. With those also came diseases."

Lydia walked outside onto the balcony and looked around the lush gardens of the palace and said softly, "I have seen the devastation, Brother. At the Queen's Hospital smallpox destroys entire families, and now we have the leprosy plague that has come from Asia. Moloka'i must be the saddest place on earth."

David leaned on the railing, "Our greatest king, King Kamehameha, used war to unite the islands. He was in Ka'ilua when Captain Cook arrived. I've heard the stories of his obsession with the Union Jack and Cook's weapons. That is why our flag looks the way it does."

"I always wondered why the British flag is on our flag. That makes sense now."

"However what still haunts me to this day, Sister, is what Kamehameha did to our relatives just a few miles from here. I never told you, but O'ahu Chief Kalanikupule was our kupuna, our grandfather. Kamehameha led a surprise attack on Waikiki and on our relatives. They fought for several days, but with rifles and cannons kupuna could only retreat up into mountains in Nu'uanu.

Kamehameha drove him, and over 700 men, off the cliff at Pali." David stared into the distance as tears fell from his big brown eyes.

He took a big deep breath, "It would take nearly 20 years of war to obtain unity and peace. I suppose, in the big picture, there has not been war between the Hawaiian people for 60 years now."

Lydia wiped away her tears and sniffed, "But Brother, you are the Merrie Monarch. You will unite all of what is remaining of us Hawaiians, from Hilo to Princeville, and keep peace without war!"

"I fear we have much more to worry about than fighting amongst ourselves. The American and Japanese businessmen are growing stronger and we are growing weaker. We need military help from some other country."

Lydia looked at the world map framed in David's office and pointed to Australia, "England started this mess, maybe they can help us end it."

Chapter 7
Rally the Union Jack
Honolulu, O'ahu, the King's Palace, October 3, 1887

Thomas Baitmen was born in London in 1852. He earned a double major in Polynesian anthropology and political science from the University of Oxford. He was the perfect man to help rally the support of the British.

Thomas was tall for his time, standing at 6 feet tall. He had a large nose and wavy blonde hair with piercing blue eyes. Making him even more odd looking was the large chip in his front tooth. His first experience eating a coconut was dreadful. No one told him not to bite the brown outside shell. However, the Hawaiian ladies found him extremely attractive; he looked so different from Hawaiian men. His Hawaiian wife, Grace Keilani Kaanapali Baitmen, came from Maui. She was a typical Hawaiian beauty, but not ordinary. A mere 5 foot tall, beautiful tan, long black wavy hair, large dark brown eyes, and her adorable smile infatuated the hearts of many men in her day. Visually they made an odd pair, but were truly deeply in love.

Thomas earned his position in Hawai'i through the British Department of War. His job was to assist the royal families with commerce to Great Britain and Australia. Ambassador Baitmen had several intimate meetings with the royal siblings, ensuring that Great Britain only meant to expand commercial intercourse with the islands, not to manipulate them in any political manner. However like the Americans, the British also had a love for sugar in their tea.

Grace Keilani was the daughter of the Maui Chief Kihei Kaanapali. Chief Kaanapali grew up in old Hawai'i. He had lived through all four King Kamehamehas. He was a traditionalist. He loved the hula, the luau, the Hawaiian gods, and customs. Yet, Chief Kaanapali understood the power of guns, machines, and medicine. An English doctor had saved his brother when a shark bit on his leg. Had it not been for modern medicine, his brother would have died. Also his armed guards had used new rifles to kill two fugitives that escaped jail and attempted to murder the chief and his family. Although he saw the usefulness of these things, the chief became worried that the western ways would change Maui in a negative way. He was right to do so.

Keilani would often travel to O'ahu with her father, Kihei, when he had meetings with King Kamehameha IV, and now with King David. Keilani and Thomas had met two years prior. Within three months of courtship, and after getting the approval of her father, the two were engaged. Chief Kaanapali did not approve at first. He did not want to lose another tradition and custom of a traditional Hawaiian wedding, and later Hawaiian children. However, King Kalākaua assured Chief Kaanapali that Thomas was an honorable and wealthy man, and he would be able to care for Keilani.

The couple wed in June on the beach of the old Whaler's Village in La'Haina. It was a traditional wedding. Every Hawaiian chief attended and so did King Kalākaua. Princess Lydia, her best friend, was the maid of honor. She was called Grace in Thomas' English circle of friends, and Keilani in her Hawaiian circle. The couple always traveled to the king's palace together. Under most circumstances Thomas would meet for business with the king, Grace would visit with the princess.

A courier bringing a request to meet secretly with King David came as a shock to both Thomas and Grace Keilani. So, late in the evening the ambassador and his wife quietly walked to the king's palace. It was 10 o'clock. The streets were pitch-dark, and the neighborhoods of Honolulu were very quiet. Just a few tiki-torches lit the perimeter of the king's palace.

As the couple arrived, Koa the guardsmen, made a silent hand gesture to the couple to walk up the stairs. The palace was barely lit. The couple walked quickly, but cautiously not to trip on some of the uneven flooring. Koa escorted them to the king's chambers. Waiting on the other side of the door were King David and Princess Lydia. They were not greeted with the typical bellowing of the king.

Both the king and princess stood and walked over to shake the ambassador's hand. Lydia embraced Keilani for what she felt was an usually long time, even for Lydia. They slowly separated and kissed each other's cheeks.

Quietly Princess Lydia whispered, "Aloha my dearest. It is so good to see you." Lydia whispered something in Hawaiian to Keilani.

Keiani's smile disappeared, "Is everything all right my friend?"

"I will let our king take it from here."

King David motioned for the couple to sit. Both he and Lydia slid their chairs as close as they could to the Baitmens. "I apologize for any fear I may have caused, but this meeting is of the utmost secrecy and importance." David looked over at Lydia, "The king and princess of Hawai'i need your help!" Then he looked back at Thomas.

Thomas and Keilani, looked at each other with confusion.

"There are probably no other people in our kingdom that we can trust with this mission."

Thomas always spoke proper English and tonight spoke quietly with his smooth English accent, "Your Majesty, I am at your service. How can I help?"

With his fingers clasped the king leaned in, "Thomas, Ambassador Baitmen, the throne is in grave danger. Two nights ago the palace was nearly overrun by 200 people with guns. Even though the princess placated the violence two nights ago, the unrest was not resolved. My sources tell me it just wasn't the Hawaiians that were behind this. There is a group of businessmen who want to take over the throne. They want the United States to annex our kingdom and make it theirs. Not only that, I also understand that some of the Japanese farmers have asked for military support from Japan. They are colluding with the Chief of Kaua'i to make that island an independent kingdom."

Thomas looked at Lydia. She sadly nodded in agreement.

"What would you have me do, Your Majesty?"

"The princess and I need military help, and we need our soldiers trained. We are hopeful you can sail to Australia where we have great support, to purchase rifles and cannons. We also need a military specialist to help with the training." The king was slightly animated.

"Of course, Your Majesty. Anything for you and Princess Lydia."

The princess spoke up, "This is what I was referring to Keilani. The king and I have a ship ready to set sail in four hours. We want it to be out of sight before light."

If his enemies saw one of the king's ships leaving, this could send a signal that the king is afraid of those who are plotting against us, whether the king is on it or not.

"If the ship is already gone, most will not even notice." Lydia put her hand on Keilani's.

David walked over to the map, "We think with my steam ship you can get to Australia in a week. I need the both of you to pack tonight and be on board by 2 am. I am sorry there is so little time."

Lydia looked at Keilani, "My dearest, I will personally tell your father when he arrives next week. With any luck you will be back by November."

King David handed Thomas a sealed letter that requested military assistance from Australia. "There will be gold, thousands of American dollars, and supplies to trade for the weapons. Plus we are also sending four of our finest guards with you."

Thomas walked over and accepted the letter, along with the responsibility. He shook the king's hand and bowed. Lydia and Keilani hugged once again. Lydia took off a necklace and placed it over Keilani's head. "May this guide and protect you, as it has done for me for many years. This necklace was given to me by Kamala, King Kamehameha III's wife. May it bring you as much luck and comfort as it has brought me."

Keilani could not speak. She just smiled, curtsied, turned and walked outside into the darkness.

The four guardsmen quietly waited outside of the ambassador's apartment. Within a few minutes the couple had four steamer trunks of clothes and secret papers ready to go.

One of the guardsmen, Tafa, slowly proceeded to lead the carriage down several blocks to the awaiting ship. The sound and smell of the steamship often gathered a crowd at the dock, curious about the latest inventions and supplies being introduced to the Hawaiian people.

Tonight however, the weather cooperated for the clandestine voyage. The winds were brisk and were directed out to sea. The noise and smoke of the engine were driven out to sea as well, and did not arouse suspension or curiosity of any villager.

The plan had worked for now. By the time the sun rose on Waikiki Beach, the king's ship, called the *Kamehameha,* was far over the horizon steadily chugging towards Sydney, Australia.

Chapter 8
Hope and Prepare
Makaha Valley, Northwest Region of O'ahu,
Nov. 20, 1887

Several kane warriors from the village of
Makaha gathered their largest canoes at the

shore. Just a few hours earlier, four guardsmen of King Kalākaua rowed ashore to alert the village soldiers. It was 3 am and they needed to work quickly. Ambassador Baitmen had completed his mission successfully in Australia and wanted to unload his supplies before daybreak.

The British government in Australia sold Thomas a significant amount of rifles, the latest Gatling guns, five canons, ammunition, and gunpowder. The British military donated three training officers to the Hawaiian king for six months to secretly train the Hawaiian military.

The plan was to unload all of the materials in Makaha. Haoles were rarely allowed to visit Makaha. Many of the villagers were traditionalists and preferred to be left alone from the westerners. They rejected technology and progress for the most part and had remained as fishermen and simple farmers of kalo and coconuts. Every now and then they would raid the haole's fields to steal some pineapples. This isolation allowed the king to secretly store and stockpile the weapons without any hostile factions becoming aware for the next several years.

The kanes from Makaha and all who were able
bodied on the king's ship, *The Kamehameha,*
unloaded the heavy shipments onto large
canoes, and rowed onto the shore where the
villagers hid the supplies in a lava tube cave
and other secret locations. The orange glow
of the morning clouds on the eastern horizon
eventually exposed the kings' vessel, but the
work had been done. If any American or
Japanese ships were in the area, they would
have seen no suspicious activity. By 8 am *the
Kamehameha* steamed back to Pearl Harbor
with the British training officers dressed as
civilians. All anyone knew was that this
mission appeared to have brought in a bounty
of meat, chickens, rice, and a pair of koalas for
King Kalākaua's personal zoo. The cover story
worked. Most people never questioned why
the king's ship had been gone.

The king's trusted guardsman, Koa, had sent
the king's carriage to pick up the British
civilians before a large crowd had gathered,
hoping to reduce the questioning of these new
arrivals. The crowd however did quickly
gather with excitement over the shipment of
beef and chickens, which were quickly
auctioned off. The word spread rapidly of

these new creatures that were to be added to the king's zoo. The local school was canceled so all of the children of Honolulu could see the curious looking koalas.

Ambassador Baitmen and his wife Grace Keilani arrived at their apartment. They were given an hour to unpack, freshen up, and report to the king. At noon, the couple arrived for a private lunch with King David and Princess Lydia. As they approached the palace, there seemed to be an extra level of excitement. It was as if everyone knew what had just been accomplished.

The ambassador and his wife walked through the king's chamber doors. To their surprise, they weren't greeted by the king, but by Keilani's father: Chief Kaanapali of Maui. "Father!" Keilani yelled as she ran into his arms. The chief picked her up off her feet and spun them both around.

"Daughter! I missed you so. How was your voyage?"

Just then a side door opened and King David bellowed, "ALOOOO HA! Please save your stories until lunch. We are extremely excited to hear from you and the ambassador about your journey to Australia."

Princess Lydia followed King David through the door and her eyes met Keilani's. Keilani curtsied and smiled. Princess Lydia motioned, "Come over here my dear. I missed you so much. I see the pendant gave you all the luck you needed."

"Yes, Your Highness." Keilani responded. "Would you like it back?"

"Oh dear no. That was a gift. Please let's all sit. Lunch is already on the table."

The king shooed away all of the staff. The group sat down to a buffet: smoked pork, poi, coconut pudding, pineapple freshly cut into squares, mangos, smoked Ahi, and scrambled eggs. The Baitmens were famished, as they had been eating ship rations for weeks. They ate with inappropriate speed. This gave the king joy to see the young couple enjoying his prepared meal.

King David tapped the corners of his mouth with his napkin. "So what is the creature you brought for my zoo? I have never seen anything quite like it."

Thomas replied, "It is called a koala, Your Majesty. It is a very slow moving creature and prefers mainly one food: eucalyptus leaves, as the Australians call them. So we brought back a month or two supply of leaves, but that will not sustain the creatures. We also brought back several young eucalyptus trees that we hope you will allow us to plant in your arboretum. We were told they require an intense amount of water. A grove of eucalyptus can actually drain a swamp. Perhaps we could plant a few in Waikiki to lower the water table there."

Princess Lydia jumped in, "Oh that's a great idea. Maybe that can reduce the swampy smell there and also reduce those pesky mosquitoes."

Chief Kaanapali interjected, "May I propose a toast to the ambassador and his successful mission!" The group raised their glasses and in unison and shouted "CHEERS!"

"Well, ambassador, if you would, please tell us about your journey."

Ambassador Baitmen looked around, "May I speak openly here, Your Majesty?"

King David put down his silverware. "Of course."

"Sir William Cairns, the Governor, was quite excited for the deal and to be able to help you. We brought back 500 rifles and thousands of rounds of ammunition. Plus we acquired the three cannons to protect Pearl Harbor and one hundred cannon balls with plenty of gunpowder. He also gave us one Gatling gun. It is hand cranked but can fire several rounds per minute. It can take the place of 20 soldiers. He also said, if needed, the British or Australian government can send more weapons on credit. Apparently the British government is anxious to get more of a trade foothold here. Governor Cairns admitted he wanted to reduce American and Japanese presence in the Hawaiian Islands."

Chief Kaanapali chimed in, "Why else do you think they want to help? Most want something in exchange."

Thomas responded, "Oh I don't think it's a secret that he trusted me because I am British; the Brits definitely would like to become better trade partners with the Hawaiians. Sugar is in high demand in England. If you are willing to purchase more weapons, they are willing to send the next ship with more cannons for Maui, the Big Island, and Kaua'i."

Chief Kaanapali spoke again, "That would be amazing! We currently have a very small arsenal to defend ourselves. If British or the Japanese were to attack us first, there would be no way to get help from you, Your Majesty, before it would be too late."

King David turned to the chief, "I agree. All our islands must be able to defend themselves from any invaders until the other island armies can come to help. I believe Emma would be interested so she could protect the Big Island, but I am not sure whether Chief Peke from Kaua'i would not use the weapons against us. He has ties to Japan, and I do not trust him."

Princess Lydia spoke up, "Perhaps, Your Majesty, a visit by me to Kaua'i is past due. I hate getting seasick, but I do have a strong relationship with the chief and his wife. I am sure he would rather have his own islanders defend him than a force from Oʻahu. We are all Hawaiians, but many of us still have allegiance to our island."

"You are brilliant, Princess. Perhaps I can send you, Ambassador Baitmen, and the lovely Keilani to combine all of your negotiation skills. I need to get all the chiefs here and start our training. I have a feeling the businessmen on our islands are growing impatient with our reluctance to become part of America. There will be a time when the American military will come to visit."

Chapter 9
Thar She Blows & Circumnavigation
Alenuihaha Channel between Maui and the
Big Island,
March 10, 1880

A decade prior….

King David had heard so many tales about the whalers that had visited the Hawaiian Islands. For decades, David had seen the whales from afar and knew of their grandeur and grace. They had almost been hunted to near extinction in both the Pacific and Atlantic Oceans. Thomas Edison's creation of the incandescent bulb with the addition of oil discoveries in Titusville, Pennsylvania, would help end the demand for whale blubber.

While walking around the new improvements of Pearl Harbor, King David ran into Captain Dan Sinclair.

"Your Majesty, it is such a pleasure to meet you in person. Are you enjoying your visit to the 'new and improved' Pearl Harbor?" Captain Dan shouted from the deck of his whaling vessel, *The Coconut*.

King David shouted back, "It is amazing! Ships are getting larger and larger. The American engineers have done a fabulous job. Progress can be great, don't you think?"

Captain Dan walked down his plank, so as not to yell at the king, "Would it be all right if we shared a meal and a few stories?"

"Oh I think that would be outstanding. I truly enjoy meeting new people and hearing their stories from around the world. I need to travel to California one day to improve our trade. Perhaps you can take me there. Is your ship fit for a cross ocean voyage?"

The two men walked until they came to a local eatery where they exchanged stories for hours. Captain Dan invited the king to come on a whaling voyage and King David accepted.

A few days later

King David could barely contain his excitement as he climbed the gangplank of *The Coconut.* The newer steam ships of this time could travel easily over ten knots. *The Coconut* reached the whales in one day's voyage.

King David asked, "How do you know where to find them?"

"Their natural migration patterns take them through the channels of the Hawaiian Islands in the winter months. Their spouts give them away from a far."

"Why are you still hunting them? It seems like almost all of the whalers are gone?"

"To be honest, Your Majesty, with the discovery of oil in Titusville, Pennsylvania in 1959, the demand for whale oil has decreased rapidly. Not only that, Thomas Edison's Light bulb will change the world. There is much less demand for oil now, but we can make a little money with the locals."

"Chief Kaanapali from Maui tells me his Whaler's Village is almost a ghost town now, and I want to meet this Thomas Edison one day."

"Oh I would have to agree. It used to be quite bustling in the winter months. Very few ships anchor there now, and Thomas Edison seems bright." Captain Dan waited for David to laugh. "See what I did there? Thomas Edison's light bulb. He was bright." Dan smiled.

King David stood there stone faced. David was torn internally during this voyage. He loved adventure, and knew some traditionalists of Hawai'i still consumed the whales. He knew that the discovery of petroleum reduced the need to slaughter the animals. He thought perhaps it was time to outlaw whaling. However, he was curious how the process happened.

It didn't take long to spot a pod of humpbacks. "THAR SHE BLOWS" yelled the spotter. The crew got right to work. They manned the harpoon boat. They quickly lowered themselves into the water. As *The Coconut* got within 100 yards, the crew started rowing in sync towards the group. Humpbacks made their annual trek to the Hawaiian Islands to birth their calves. Full-grown adult humpbacks were nearly as long as Captain Dan's Ship. The king wondered how the crew would get one on board. He would soon find out.

Captain Sinclair pointed out to the pod, "The pod behaves much like *pipis* or cows do on the islands. They move very slowly. They move as a group just as if they were grazing. If the wind stops blowing you can hear some of them make noise."

"WUUUUUUUUU" The whales seemed to moan a hello to the harpoon boat. Their tails would breach and splash. Some of them stuck up their flippers as if they were waving hello. Periodically, one would breach. As if in slow motion, a 35 foot whale threw itself out of the water. Then it fell gracefully back into the ocean as its fluke made a thunderous crashing sound on the turquoise water. The king thought these were the most incredible creatures on planet earth.

The king asked Captain Sinclair, "So what happens now?"

"The crew will row until they are right on top of the whale. It's quite easy. The whales don't try to swim away or dive. Unfortunately for them, they are so large they have no natural predators and aren't afraid of us. The harpooner will throw two or three harpoons into the side of one. It usually takes some time until they are too exhausted to swim and then we row it to the ship and start processing it."

"Process it? What does that entail?"

"Oh it's a bloody mess. We cut it to pieces to get it up onto the ship. Then we separate the blubber, the meat, and the organs. We will try to process as much as possible." We sell the blubber to America, and the meat to the Japanese, and the organs to the Hawaiians."

King David watched as the harpooner stood up. David could see they were directly on top of a whale, and just as the captain had said, the whales were unaware of the danger. Easy prey. The harpoon was released. The whale let out a loud "WUUUUUUUUUUU!" Still it barely struggled. The second harpooner let loose the next harpoon, and the two rowboats started to drag the whale away from its family.

King David watched as the Coconut closed in on the wounded animal. The whale was still alive. Its tail flipped up and down a few times. It moaned a few more times. The king would never forget as the humpback rolled slightly to its side one last time, and their eyes met. He could sense the whale's pain as the exhausted creature slowly closed its eye for the last time as it bled out.

King David lowered his head in shame and thought, "How could we do this to these magnificent beings? I pray the gods will forgive us."

And as if Pele herself heard his prayer, Mauna Loa erupted with a bang so loud all aboard fell to the deck.

"Captain Sinclair, Pele is angry. I think we should leave!" the king warned.

Captain Sinclair stood up and looked at the volcano just a few miles in the distance, "Jesus, Mary, and Joseph! Men! We need to process this whale in the next 30 minutes and get the hell out of here!"

The men were frightened, having never seen a volcano explode before. They worked faster than they'd ever worked. It would have been a waste of that magnificent whale to let it go. So they cut it into pieces in minutes and let much of it sink to the bottom of Alenuihaha Channel. The ash and rock were slowly starting to fall into the ocean around them. They could see canoes rowing towards them from the island. There was no room on board for the islanders now. The deck was covered with blood, blubber, and whale organs.

Captain Dan Sinclair fired up the engine and *the Coconut* set off full steam to the west to get some distance from the volcanic debris.

As soon as King David returned to his palace, he told his story to Princess Lydia. He quickly wrote a proclamation making it illegal to hunt whales in Hawaiian waters.

Later that year, King David wanted to make history, and he did. He wanted to be the first king in the history of the world to circumnavigate the globe. In 1881 King David set sail with his two best friends William Armstrong and Charles Judd and began to sail around the world.

A tearful Aloha left Princess Lydia as Regent in charge of the islands as David left for months. His goals were to recruit labor and business for Hawai'i.

David made his way to California then across the Pacific to Japan and China, and then to India and Europe. After several months, King David ended up in Washington D.C. where he met with President Arthur. It was King David's second meeting with a president as he met with President Grant years' prior. Before his transcontinental train ride, David also met with Thomas Edison. The two made plans to bring electricity to Iolani Palace.

Chapter 10
The Yamamotos
Tokyo, March 1, 1891

A decade later ...

The cherry blossoms covered the trees that lined the streets of Tokyo. It was spring and the weather was getting warmer. As Haruto and Sakura Yamamoto walked down Main Street, they were discussing the name of their next child. Sakura was showing and excited, yet had a few months to go. A young Hideki was holding his mother's hand. The parents took their time so his little legs could keep up. Sakura stopped and pointed to Mt. Fuji. It still had plenty of winter snow at its summit.

Haruto was concerned about the speed in which their world was changing, and was unsure he wanted his children to be raised in the "new" Japan.

As Haruto continued to walk he fell silent, he remembered the story from his father of the first time his dad saw westerners. He told the story of Commodore Matthew Perry of the US Navy. Perry sailed his fleet into Tokyo Bay in 1853, which broke 220 years of political isolation. For centuries, tradition held a firm grip of feudal Japan. That all changed when Perry sailed into Tokyo Bay.

As a young man, Haruto watched his country change as the Meiji Era and the Industrial Revolution began. The technology and the progress of machines divided his government, his culture, and his family.

He remembered how heartbroken his father was when he told Haruto of his heroes; the Samurai. Their old ways of fighting with honor and the study of martial arts were coming to an end. Japan's simple existence, traditional farm and warrior life, was ending. In 1873 Haruto's father witnessed how Itagaki Taisuke proposed a constitutional monarchy, stripping the emperor of what the Japanese believed was a god given power. Haruto's final epiphany came in 1885, when Japanese poet Yukichi Fukuzawa wrote a popular essay, *Leaving Asia.*

The Yamamoto family was being torn apart. Fukuzawa's essay struck home with Haruto. He yearned for a simple life. Where once were tiny cottages and farms, now large factories spewed smoke. The sweet fragrances of the spring blossoms were now overpowered with coal smoke. The quiet streets of his neighborhood became louder each passing day with horses and carriages hauling large amounts of cotton and yarn. Revealing Haruto's plan to leave Asia created constant bickering with his father. Although Haruto's father was saddened by the downside of progress, he refused to leave Japan.

Haruto received a letter from his cousin in Haleiwa, Hawai'i. He was doing well and in need of farmers and businessmen. Haruto was both. He made up his mind, and with Sakura's support, they decided to sell what they could and start a new life in the kingdom of Hawai'i. It was still a long, treacherous voyage with the newest ships, but worth the risk in Haruto's eyes.

When Haruto eventually got the courage to tell his father his plan, Haruto's father yelled, "You are taking my grandchildren away from me and your mother! How could you do this to us?" Haruto's mother cried into her hands. Sakura put her arm around Grandma's shoulder.

"Father, I know you don't like the change Japan is experiencing either. You can still come with us. You've told me many times of how Japan is changing for the worse. There is still enough time to sell the house and pack. We leave in three days! Father, Hawai'i is warm. You'll never have to be cold again!"

Haruto's father stuck out his palm towards Haruto, "Enough! I have nothing to say to you. You shame me, and your mother! You are selfish and hurtful. First off, you began attending that Christian church. Now you are leaving your homeland. You are a disgrace to us and JAPAN! Do as you please. Just know, once you walk out that door, you will NEVER see us again!"

Haruto bowed, then motioned for Sakura to go into their private quarters and finish packing. Quietly he whispered to Sakura, "He can be so damn stubborn. I know he says those things because he is hurting, but they both could be comfortable in Hawai'i in their elder years. He just will not listen."

The day to leave came. Haruto stood in the doorway waiting for his parents to turn to him to say sayonara. They would not look. They stood silent, looking out of the window. Their hearts were breaking, but they had too much pride to turn and hug their only son farewell. Haruto closed the door and the small family walked to the port to catch their ship. As Haruto was walking up the plank, he turned to see the thousands of beautiful cherry blossoms on the trees and Mt. Fuji for the last time. However his last memories of Japan would be the smoke that hovered over his once pristine city.

Three days had passed when a crewmember walked through the main hallways knocking on doors. "A storm is approaching! Close your port windows immediately!"

Within minutes, the ship was swaying side to side. Over and over the front of the ship rose several feet, then sank several feet back down. After several minutes of this torture, Sakura became extremely ill. "Haruto, I must get fresh air. I am suffocating in here!" She yelled as she ran out of the door.

"Hideki! Stay here!" Haruto yelled to his young son as he ran after Sakura. The ship tossed violently sideways and Haruto fell to the ground. "SAKURA! Come back!" She had already made it to the top deck. Haruto struggled to climb the ladder, which took him to the top deck. He made it through the door and was slapped in the face with the storm surge.

He could see Sakura a few yards ahead. "SAKURA!"

Sakura was hanging onto the rail and vomiting over the side. The ship rolled to the right and Sakura looked back at Haruto. A large wave crashed over the deck. Haruto hung on to the rail with his strong arms. When the water subsided. Sakura was gone!

Haruto ran to the railing and saw Sakura. She had somehow grabbed onto a buoy that had also fallen overboard. The current was so strong it was lifting her up a mountain of ocean like a kite pulling a bow. Haruto yelled as loud as he could, but the storm was so loud he couldn't hear his own screams. Sakura continued to rise up the wall of water until she reached the peak, then dipped behind the storm surge.

Haruto struggled to get to the control room. A sailor inside saw him through a window. "Captain! There's a man outside!"

The captain rushed to learn what Haruto was doing on the deck, "Good god man what are you doing?"

"My wife fell overboard! We must try to save her!"

The captain simply said, "I am sorry sir. She is lost." Haruto pleaded for the slight chance of finding Sukuro, yet the captain refused to turn around. Haruto dropped to his knees and wept.

In time, the storm passed. The ship, along with its cargo and passengers sailed into Haleiwa port. The sky was light blue. The hills were covered in a brilliant green from the sugar cane and pineapples. Hawaiians came to the pier to greet the new arrivals and to see what was in the cargo hold.

Most of the passengers had disembarked. Haruto's cousin, Aiko was waiting patiently on the pier. He saw Haruto and Hideki walking down the plank and began to wave ecstatically and shouted "Haruto! Haruto! Over here!"

Haruto needed help with his second piece of luggage. Aiko ran up part of the gangplank and looked over Haruto's shoulder. Aiko asked, "Where's Sakura?" as he picked up Hideki.

Quietly Haruto said, "There was a storm… and Sakura went up top because she was ill and… and… a wave took her, Aiko."

Aiko stood motionless in shock, holding Hideki. The boy asked softly, "Where's momma?" The men hugged each other and cried.

The mourning became easier with time, and Haruto began to assist in Aiko's small fruit business and farm. He had worked tirelessly to make it profitable. The two men talked daily about getting a much larger farm, like in Japan. Living in O'ahu made that dream nearly impossible. The best land had already been purchased. However, the fruit stand they had was profitable. When ships came in, crewmembers would buy out most of their produce. They earned enough cash to improve the store and hire more employees. Their fruit stand eventually, turned into a grocery store.

In time, young Hideki became a very good student and a hard worker in the fields. Haruto gave him Sundays off to go to the new protestant church and rest. However, without a mother, the daily chores of keeping house became a burden.

Aiko, Haruto, and Hideki sat at the dinner table one evening.

Hideki was just seven, "Father, I mean no disrespect, but I am exhausted every day. I go to school, I get good grades and I work in the fields or at the store. My friend Johnny told me they hired a Chinese helper to assist with the chores. Can we buy one too?"

Aiko and Haruto looked at each other and chuckled, "Well son, I do appreciate all that you do. I know you work hard, but we don't 'buy' people. We could pay people to do some work for us. Having no women in the house does make life a little more difficult. I tell you what, pray for God to help us." Hideki looked at Aiko.

Hideki asked, "Cousin Aiko, why don't you have a wife?"

Haruto smiled and asked, "Yes, Aiko, why DON'T you have a wife?"

Aiko put down his chopsticks, "Well, if I must be honest, I'm waiting for the right one to come along. Have you seen the women of Haleiwa? YUCK!" The men laughed. Hideki wasn't sure why. "I want one of those beauties from Honolulu. Now there are some beautiful women there."

There was a knock at the door and the men turned their heads. "Who could that be?" Aiko asked as he got up and answered the door. A short Chinese man with a small boy were standing on the front steps. Behind them were a woman and a young girl. The sunshine hit Aiko's eyes and he placed his hand up to shield the rays. "May I help you?"

Ho's English vocabulary was impressive, but his speech was broken, "Hello. My name is Ho San. My family just came from Hong Kong and we are in need of money. I would like to know if you need a servant. My son, Po San, will do anything you need. For only five dollars a month, he can be yours."

Aiko looked back at Haruto. Haruto looked back at Hideki. He had a huge smile and looked up to the sky, clasped his hands, and said, "Thank you, thank you, thank you."

Haruto and Hideki walked over to the door to see the new help. Hideki said "Hello", but Po just looked down in shame. His father was selling him for five dollars. "Father, can we buy him?"

"Son, what did I tell you? We do not buy people!"

Aiko looked at Haruto, "Well, he could keep the house clean, help at the store, and even in the fields. What do you say?"

We could afford five dollars a month, and that would give you more time to find a wife."
Haruto smiled.

"Ok Mr. Ho San; it is a deal. Let me go get your five dollars." Ho looked back and smiled at his wife and daughter. They were not happy and did not smile back.

Aiko came back to the door, "Here you go Mr. Ho San, five silver dollars. I will arrange at the Bank of Hawai'i on Main Street for you to receive five dollars at the first of each month."

He bowed, said "thank you", and bowed again.

Po slowly walked back up to the porch, and in very broken English asked, "What do you want me to do?"

Haruto said, "Why don't you join us for dinner and you can start tomorrow."

"I can eat? Po suddenly had a smile.

"Yes Po, you can eat. And it looks like with this arrangement, your family can now too. This will not be easy. We will expect you to work hard, but we will feed you and take care of you." Haruto said sternly.

Chapter 11
The Sans
Hong Kong, 1896

Ko San jumped out of the way of a charging rickshaw. Ko was still pretty agile for having fifty trips around the sun. The streets of Hong Kong had become extremely busy and violent lately. Since the British increased their desire to colonize Hong Kong, businesses exploded with activity in the streets. With new businesses came thousands of Chinese from the countryside. People in the countryside were starving. They came to dig ditches. They came to clean homes. They came to pull rickshaws. The Sans were losing their sense of community. Ko did not like the new Hong Kong.

He walked into his apartment. "Hello everyone."

The family responded, "Hello father."

"I have big news! I talked to my boss today down on the dock. He told me they are expanding their company to Hawai'i. He wants me to help him start up his company there. I think I want to go."

The family all began to ask questions simultaneously, "What?" "Where is Hawai'i? When will you leave? I don't understand?"

"Wait everybody. Let me explain. Mr. Chow has a shipping company and they have a ship that goes to tropical islands and brings back fruit to Hong Kong. The British have helped finance this new venture. I don't like the way Hong Kong is progressing. The progress brought by the British is slowly changing our way of life."

His son Ho inquired, "How long will you be gone Father?"

"I plan on staying, and I want you to come with me."

"Father, we have no money for the voyage."

"Mr. Chow said that, "I can take my entire family for free. He will even feed you during the week's journey as well!"

"Honestly Father, there is nothing here for us either. If it weren't for you, Po and Jo would starve. We will go with you, Father." Ho looked at his wife and children for reassurance. "When would we leave?"

"Next week."

"That's so soon." He looked again at his wife, "Honey, I don't like the new Hong Kong either. We have nothing here any more. I think I want to go."

Su smiled, "Where you go, we go."

The British cargo ship loaded its hold with supplies for the Hawaiian Railroad, a couple of tractors, tons of rice, and 100 pigs. Added to that were 20 Chinese laborers and three lepers bound for Moloka'i.

The British government felt it was more civilized to have the lepers live with their own kind and pay the Hawaiians to care for them. Also on board were four British businessmen who had made the agreement with Mr. Chow to have Ho's father help his boss run the business.

The voyage was fairly uneventful. The San's children, Jo and Po, became bored quickly after the excitement of the trip wore off. The few children on board kept busy by playing creative games with sticks and marbles. One morning a few pigs got loose and the passengers were entertained watching the crew try to recapture wild pigs.

The ship blew its horn to signal to Haleiwa they were approaching. It also awoke the passengers. Most of the immigrants slept on the floor of an overcrowded cabin.

A crew-member walked through the corridor yelling, "Remain in your cabins. The Hawaiian military will come to inspect every cabin before you are allowed to enter Hawai'i. Remain in your cabins!"

Ho and his wife looked at each other Ho commented. "Well Honey, it looks like things are starting to finally turn around for us. We are going to have jobs and a place to stay."

She smiled, "Yes my dear. Confucius would say, 'fish must swim together, or the stresses of life will separate them'. I am happy to swim next to you."

Po had been sleeping on the floor next to Ko. He crawled over to his parents,
"Father! Grandpa won't wake up!"

Twenty minutes later the British businessmen came down to the cabin where Mr. San had just passed away. "I regret the loss of your father, Ho. Do you know anything about running our business?"

"No Sir, I was planning on being a laborer for my father." Ho tried to hold back his tears.

"Oh dear, that is unfortunate. I have plenty of laborers. What I need is a plant manager. We are definitely in a pickle. Unfortunately my good man, we will have no need for your services." They left the Sans to mourn for their father.

To make matters worse, the captain informed the Sans that to remove and bury their father would cost ten American dollars.

"We have no money!" Ho sobbed.

"I tell you what I will do for you, Ho. On our journey back, we will bury him at sea for no cost." The captain motioned for some workers to move the body.

Distraught, the small family of four walked the streets of Haleiwa. They could not read English or Hawaiian. Ho and Po could speak a little English. By the time they got off the ship, all of the Chinese passengers had left for their destinations. They were lost in a foreign land, with no money, no job, and no place to stay.

Ho looked at Su, "I know what I must do." It was evening now and they had not eaten in 24 hours. Ho walked until he saw a house that looked like wealthy people lived in it. He grabbed Po's hand and led him up to the door.

A Japanese man opened the door. The sun hit the Japanese man in the eye, he raised his hand to shade his view, and looked over Ho's shoulder to see Su and Jo.

"May I help you?" The Japanese man said in English.

"Hello, my name is Ho San. My family just came from Hong Kong. We have run into a terrible situation, and we are in need of money. I would like to know if you need a servant? My son Po San will do anything you need. For only five dollars a month, he can be yours."

Another Japanese man and a boy came to the door. The boy said, "Hello" to Po, but he just looked down in shame. The boy asked if he could buy Po. Ho was extremely ashamed, but could not think of a better solution.

"I suppose it is not permanent, and we would like to visit once a month, and then I will come by to collect my fee, if that's ok with you?" The two men discussed it; one man said he'd go get the five dollars. Ho looked back and smiled at Su, but she didn't smile back.

"I would like a word with my son if I may?"

Ho leaned over and spoke in Cantonese, "Son. Listen. Your mother and I love you, but at least here, you will have a roof over your head. These people have money. You will be fed. We will come by to visit once a month. I promise!" Po said nothing. He ran to his mother and sister to hug them goodbye.

The man then told Ho he would set up an account at the Bank of Hawai'i and there would be five dollars waiting for him each month.

Ho walked up to his crying wife, "Honey look! Five dollars! We can get a room and a meal tonight. This should last us a few days until we can get jobs." The family walked towards downtown. "You and Jo can start your cleaning service tomorrow, and I will find work in the fields. "

Jo cried, " I miss him already."

Chapter 12
The Fourth of July
The King's Garden, Honolulu, July 4, 1898

Two years later …

Lizzy and Princess Maili were sitting criss-cross applesauce in the king's garden. It was the 4th of July. Most of the people of Hawai'i were taking advantage of the holiday. The girls were about to have their first political debate.

"Princess", Lizzy questioned, "are we going to celebrate the 4th of July like many of the other people?"

"I don't believe it would be appropriate for the princess of Hawai'i to participate in a holiday celebrating American freedom when those same Americans are trying to take freedom from the Hawaiian people; at least that's what Queen Lydia said."

"Well they are at the beach eating barbecued pork and watermelon. I love watermelon." Lizzy was whining a bit.

"As a Hawaiian, I think it would be inappropriate." The princess was trying to sound like a royal.

Lizzy was getting a little sassy, "You know it's kinda funny Your Majesty, weren't you born in America? So doesn't that make you an American?"

"As the queen would say, that was happenstance. I am Hawaiian. I am the granddaughter of Chief Kaanapali of Maui and heir to the throne."

"Well tell me Princess Maili, who is Kanehekili?"

"He does not concern me, therefore I don't care." The princess stuck her nose in the air.

"So you don't know the Hawaiian God of Thunder ehh? How about Pele?" Lizzy shot back.

"Oh everybody knows Pele. So what?"

"I think it's funny that you were born in America. You speak English. Your father is British, and you don't know Hawaiian culture or the language. I'M more Hawaiian than you!"

"HOW DARE YOU ELIZABETH DOEL! I am the heir to the throne. I should have the guards chop off your head for such … for such petulance!"

"Well Princess, I was born in Honolulu. I speak Hawaiian! I know all about Hawaiian culture and history!"

Maili stood up. She'd never been angry at Lizzy before, "You take that back Elizabeth Doel!"

Lizzy stood up. She was taller than Maili. "Or what?" and then in Hawaiian she shouted, " *HE HUPO 'OE*!" You are stupid!

Koa began walking over to the girls as he could tell this was about to get violent, "Lizzy! Don't EVER talk to the princess like that again. I know what that means!"

"Well she thinks she's more Hawaiian than me. And I strongly disagree!" She crossed her arms and huffed.

Koa was a large man and towered over Lizzy. He too crossed his tattooed arms. Koa preferred outside duty where he could wear much less clothing, which was made traditionally of tree leaves. "Unfortunately you do not have Hawaiian blood and she does."

Maili stuck her tongue out at Lizzy. "See!"

Koa took a knee and put his large brown hand on Maili's shoulder, "With all due respect Princess, Lizzy has a point too."

Lizzy stuck out her tongue in response.

"As future queen, you should know her people's language thoroughly, all aspects of culture, and our history. The Hawaiian people will need you to protect those things one day from evil forces who will try to take it all from us."

"Who would want to do such things?" asked Maili.

Koa responded, "Just look around, Princess. The Americans. The British. The Japanese. They all want to take advantage of us. One day, Princess, you will be queen of all of the Hawaiian Islands, the Hawaiian people, the lepers in Moloka'i, and even the Menehune people! It will be your responsibility that our history be preserved. It must be taught in schools so the children will not forget about the lei, the hula, the luau, and our gods. I know Queen Lili'oukalani wants this from you. So, maybe there is a little truth in Miss Elizabeth's words."

Maili just looked at the ground in shame.

"So I think you both owe each other an apology. You are too good of friends to argue over such things. Now hug."

The girls slinked over to each other and said, "Oooookay." Then they offered each other a pretend hug. Maili gave Lizzy a raspberry on her cheek and ran away laughing.

Koa looked at Lizzy, "Well? Go chase her!" Lizzy ran after her best friend as she laughed out loud.

Later that afternoon in Waikiki…

Hideki and Po were sitting under a palm tree, just feet from the shore. It was a hot, but beautiful day in Waikiki Beach. The boys were watching all of the American families picnicking on the warm sand.

Po asked, "Why are there so many haoles here today? It's a Tuesday."

"It's the 4th of July." Hideki said as he stared off at the families having fun.

"So what. Tomorrow is the 5th of July."

Hideki turned slowly to Po, "Hey Dum Dum. It's the Americans' Independence Day. They celebrate on July 4. Thomas Jefferson wrote the Declaration of Independence. They fought the British and gained their independence. They celebrate by picnicking and lighting off fireworks tonight."

Po got excited, "WOW! I love fireworks. Can we stay?"

"I'm getting hungry Po. I think we should head back soon." Hideki continued to stare again. He could see families playing in the surf and eating sandwiches. Behind them was the majestic Diamond Head. The top of the extinct volcano dominated the horizon. It reminded him of Mt. Fuji back in Japan except the top of Diamond Head had blown off. "I miss my family." Hideki's voice trailed off.

"Hideki? Do you want to get into the water?"

"NAH, My sores still hurt a little."

"They look like they are almost healed." Po stared up at Hideki for a second, pondering whether or not to ask, "Pardon me for asking, but how did your mom die?"

"On our voyage to Hawai'i, we were about three days in. We sailed into a horrible storm. The ship was rocking so badly. Everyone was scared. I thought it was exciting. My mom became seasick and didn't want to vomit in front of the other passengers. She told my father she was going topside. He told her not to go, but she started climbing up the stairs to get up on the top deck. My father chased her but fell as a wave rocked the ship again. My father climbed up as fast as he could to get her. He said he yelled at her but the storm was too loud. She grabbed the railing to lean over to throw up, and then a huge wave swept over the boat. My Father hung on for dear life. When the wave vanished... she was gone. She was pregnant with my little brother."

"How do you know it was a boy?"

"Apparently women know such things. So I guess you can be my little brother now, Po."

"That would be fine by me. My older sister has gone to Moloka'i. I don't have any brothers. I would like that. A lot!" Po smiled.

"Ok, but you still have to do as I tell you!"

"Yes Sir." Po saluted, "I mean yes brother."

"Let's not get carried away Po."

The two boys took one last look at the American families having fun, and walked back to Iolani Palace. It was getting late in the afternoon when they arrived. They were both famished from a long hot day of walking in the sun, and they appeared exhausted.

Koa Shouted, "Hey you keikis! You looked thirsty. Come over here and get some watermelon and lemonade."

The boys suddenly got a burst of energy and ran over to the guard's table.

"What is that?" Po asked.

Koa replied, "It is watermelon; fresh from California. Try it."

Po and Hideki were starving and dug in. They both thought it was delicious. Po asked, "Can I eat the seeds?"

Koa teased, "You can, but if you don't clean behind your ears, a watermelon will grow there!"

Po's eyes got big and he rubbed behind his ears.

The four children were allowed to stay up late to watch the American's fireworks from the palace balcony. They leaned against the rail with wonder as they watched firework shows all over Honolulu. It was the best 4th of July they'd ever had.

Chapter 13
Summer of 1899
Iolani Palace, August 19, 1899

The days of summer vacation were coming to an end. The four friends had become close. Most early mornings included running around the palace gardens and a pick up game of the new sport of baseball. The surf in Waikiki in the summer can allow a good surfer the ability to ride the two to three foot swells. The better surfers would try to get to Sandy Beach where five to ten foot swells violently crash onto the soft sands just east of Hanauma Bay. If the surf was quiet, Po and Hideki would sometimes head to the beach in the afternoon.

Po would often ask, "Hideki, is it ok if I play with the princess? She knows I'm your servant right?"

The princess and Lizzy were in earshot, "Of course it is, you silly. You are one of my best friends, Po!"

Po's eyes opened wide and he smiled, "ME?"

Princess Maili responded, "Certainly. You, Hideki, and of course, Lizzy. Remember you did kinda save my life!"

Hideki wasn't too happy with those words. He knew he was the real hero and didn't appreciate Po sharing the credit. Hideki often asked himself, "Why do I even take my servant to play with me?" But he loved Po like a little brother, even though he was jealous the girls gave Po some attention.

Hideki had a crush on both girls. But his shyness kept him from expressing his feelings. He often dreamt of marrying the princess and then one day being king of Hawai'i. He thought, "I bet my father would be proud of me then!"

Three of the children had birthdays over the summer. Hideki was the oldest. He turned 10. Lizzy was about to turn 9, along with Po. Maili would turn 9 years old in December. Hideki was quite muscular for just 10 years old. His days working out in the fields made him strong. Po was small for his age. Only weighing 80 pounds allowed him to run as fast as any child in Hawai'i. He wore torn pants that went beyond his knees and seldom wore shoes. Living with Hideki allowed him the luxury of a weekly bath. He really wasn't interested in girls yet like Hideki. Lizzy had bright blue eyes. They stood out against her Hawaiian tan and long light brown hair. Maili had big, dark brown eyes. When she smiled at Po and Hideki, their hearts melted. Both girls were tall for their age, which intimidated Hideki. All four of the children caught the eyes of the locals as they ran and played all day long on the palace grounds.

The four kids were walking in the garden when Maili stopped to pick two plumeria blossoms off the trees. She placed one on Lizzy's right ear and one on hers.

"Do you know why they are over our right ears?" Maili asked the boys.

Po shouted, "Because you're right handed!"

Lizzy laughed out loud, "Po you are so silly sometimes! Do you know Hideki?"

Hideki didn't want to appear stupid, so he just shook his head.

Lizzy walked in a circle around them and teased the boys, "Well boys, if you wear it over your right ear then you are available. If you wear it over your left, you are taken. Kinda like a wedding ring."

Po asked, "Available for what?"

The girls giggled and Maili whispered, "You know, boyfriends." And they giggled again.

Po asked naively, "Aren't we your boyfriends?"

The girls put their hands over their mouths in shock. Lizzy responded, "Oh dear no. You are our friends, and you are boys, but no are most definitely NOT our boyfriends! We like older men."

Hideki shot back, "I'm older!"

Maili put her hand on his shoulder, "Listen Hideki, you are barely 10. We are looking for mature men of at least 11 or 12."

Hideki's feelings were hurt and he started to walk away.

"Hideki! Where are you going? We are just teasing. We want your last day to be fun."

"I can't help my age!" he was sulking, "What do you mean, last day?"

Maili walked over to him sadly, "Oh, I guess no one has told you. You have to go back to Kaua'i with Po for school tomorrow."

"What? You're right! No one told me. That's crap!"

Po spoke up, "Hideki, I don't mean to correct you, but you shouldn't curse in front of the princess." Hideki punched Po's shoulder.

"OW! That hurt." Po rubbed his arm.

Maili pointed at Hideki, "Now you apologize for striking Po. He's right. You shouldn't curse in the presence of royalty."

"Oh brother." Hideki said sarcastically, "I'm sorry Po." Then whispered, "You're gonna get it later."

Lizzy put her index finger on her mouth, "Hey Hideki, I just thought of something. When we were on the beach in Kaua'i, you told me you saw something in the cave. What did you see?"

Hideki stood up straight, "Oh gee, I forgot about that. You know after saving the princess and all." he smiled.

Po ran over and patted him on the back, "Hideki is a hero, and he's my best friend."

Hideki looked down at Po with an irritated look, "From what I remember, after saving the princess, I braced my feet against the cliff because another wave was coming. I saw some movement from the mouth of the cave. It was quick, but I know I saw a person

138

looking at me. He looked like a little man. Weird huh?"

Maili ran over and shouted, "YOU SAW A MENEHUNE!"

Po asked, "A whoody whaddy?"

Maili shouted, "You know! A Menehune! The 'magical' little people of Hawai'i!" Maili was teasing because she was not truly convinced the Menehune really existed.

Lizzy spoke up, "Well Hawaiian legend says when the first Polynesians came to Kaua'i, there were fish ponds from cut lava stones already there!"

Hideki asked, "Well, if the Polynesians were the first ones, who built the fishponds?"

Lizzy replied, "That is the great mystery. Locals say they rarely see them, and they work at night. Villagers often see the work they did the next morning."

Maili crossed her arms, doubting the stories. "I'm still not sure such little people could do all of that. Let's go ask Koa!"

The children walked over to Koa, and Hideki told their favorite guard their story.

"Oh Cuzin', you saw a Menehune!"

Maili said, "Oh so you believe in the little people too?"

Koa turned to the princess, "Of course I do Princess Maili. Hawaiians have spoken of them for generations. I don't believe our ancestors would lie, do you?"

Lizzy said, "I believe!"

Po said, "Me too!"

Hideki shot back, "Of course they are real. I saw one!"

Maili crossed her arms again. She was desperately wanted proof the Menehune were real. "Hmmmm. Well next summer we will have to go back and see for ourselves!"

Koa kneeled and put his large hand on her shoulder, "Please Princess, tread lightly around the Menehune. They are known to be naughty and mischievous! They don't want to be bothered for a reason."

"Well, I will tell them that I am their princess. They must come out of the cave by royal decree!"

Koa shook his head, "Good luck with that Princess."

Maili curled her pointer finger at the kids. The kids gathered around her, "Let's promise that for the rest of our lives we will spend summers together." The children pinky swore and enjoyed every moment of their last day of summer.

Chapter 14

Jo and Noko
Kalaupapa, Moloka'i, August 20, 1899

Jo would often pinch herself and think, "Is this real?" Jo couldn't believe how amazing Kalaupapa actually was. Back home Jo had to work all day doing chores during the summer days. Even when school was over, Jo had to work for hours cleaning with her mother. Here at Kalaupapa she only had to keep her room clean. The rest of the day she could play with all of the children of the village.

Jo's new best friend was Noko. She was a 12 year old Hawaiian girl. They sat under a tall palm tree that had a large cluster of leaves at the top. They looked out into the rough waves that crashed mightily onto the rocks of the peninsula. The leaves of the palm tree gave them periodic shade as it swayed in the wind. They were quiet for a moment, tired from the run in the thick sand down to the beach. After wiggling their bottoms into the warm sand, Jo said, "Noko….. I miss my family."

"I miss mine too." Noko replied. "But you know what? I've never been happier. Is that wrong for me to say?"

"Oh my goodness, I was just thinking the same thing. I hated life back home, but love my family so much! I still cry myself to sleep some nights. I was never allowed to play at home; there was always work to do. I miss spending time with my mother, but here I get to go to the beach. I eat really yummy food. All the people here treat me kindly. It's crazy." Suddenly Jo jumped to her feet, "Noko Look! She pointed out to the ocean. A humpback whale breached and made a huge splash. "WOOOW!" the girls yelled simultaneously.

Jo said, "I've never seen one jump like that before."

Noko sighed, returning to their previous conversation, "I miss my mother too. I hate my father. He was stuck in the old world. He hated all haoles and new inventions. He would always say things were so much better when we lived the ....", she made air quotes, "traditional ways". "The traditional ways meant he sits around all day drinking rum while mom works."

Jo swiped her hair away from her mouth, "My parents immigrated from China. They rarely spoke of the old country. When they did it didn't sound so great. They said it was overcrowded, it stunk, and had a lot of crime. I came here thinking it was going to be the worst thing in the world, and it has become paradise. I really love it here, besides all of the hideous looking people."

"Jo! That's not very nice. You may look like them one day."

"You have to admit it takes a lot to get used to."

"I have only been here a year, but yes it did take some getting used to. Speaking of sores. Mine is on my back. You wanna see?"

Jo said, "Sure I guess." Noko pulled up her shirt. "It's pretty big. It's like the size of a... guava."

Noko sighed, "Yeah, it's kinda growing."

Where is yours?"

Jo pulled up her shorts, "Right here. It can barely be seen, but my teacher, Mrs. Appleton, saw it and turned me in. I couldn't believe she did that. I thought she liked me."

"Well my neighbor turned me in. The little pervert was watching me change through my window. I heard him shout, "Noko's a leper! Noko's a leper!" The next thing you know, I'm on a ship to Moloka'i. I was angry and scared at first, but now I love it here too. How is Sister Dorothy treating you?"

"Oh she's great. She's so little and cute, shuffling around all of the time. All she does is talk and cook. The only bad thing is she makes me inspect her feet. YUCK!"

Noko thought for a second, "I wonder if her feet were chopped off, would it continue to spread. Wouldn't that be the smart thing to do?"

"Well I'm not a doctor, but I hear that Hansen's disease is all over your body on the inside, and it just comes out in sores anywhere. I think it'll eventually kill us all."

Noko hmmmed, "Hey have you seen any of the poor souls that they've taken to the hospital? They are totally covered with the sores. I guess if you can't feel it, it must not be too bad."

"I have a question, Noko. If someone touches you with their infected skin, will they spread it more to you?"

"Our doctor said Hawaiian and Asian people are getting it because we eat together without silverware. We share saliva with our chopsticks and our hands when we eat family style. Once you get it, it takes its natural course. So I suppose if you don't kiss anyone, or eat family style, you should live a long life. I've seen some of my friends' sores spread quickly. Yet mine hasn't spread much at all. Hopefully both you and I will have many summers playing together."

Jo looked into her eyes, "Pinky swear?"

"Pinky swear."

Jo looked north onto the horizon. She could see thunderclouds. The ocean breeze changed directions and started to blow sand in their faces. "Maybe we should head back before we get a mouthful of sand?"

"Hey look!" Noko pointed to the rocks. Two large crabs looked like they were sword fighting with their claws.

"Hey Noko, what is school like here?"

"Oh a lot like home. However, the nuns run class. They are … pretty strict. They will swat you with a ruler if you don't pay attention. Sometimes it's just blah blah blah stuff. They let us write stories in English class, so that's my favorite."

"What do you write about Noko?"

"Oh, mostly about fantasies. I feel like another person when I'm writing about dragons and people from the sea." Noko said.

"I like to daydream about stuff like that. It makes me forget about my future. I'm sad I will never get married or have children." Jo became somber.

"How do you know that? Maybe they will find a cure someday. Modern medicine is quickly advancing. I'd give the skin off my back to find a cure."

"Ha! I get it! The skin off your back!" Jo laughed out loud. "You're funny Noko."

"Hey you might as well have a sense of humor about it. I don't want to be like these grumpy old people. That's all they talk about. I want to enjoy every day I have. The last thing my mom told me was that only I could choose my attitude. I think of that all the time. I choose to be happy! How about you Jo?"

"I never really thought about that Noko. I think I'm happy most of the time, except when I have to inspect Dorothy's feet." Jo pretended to throw up.

Noko laughed, "So let's make another pinky promise. Let's promise to be happy everyday!"

"I like that! I like that a lot, Noko."

Chapter 15
The Hawaiian League
Honolulu, O'ahu, January 10, 1887

A decade prior …

For several years, American businessmen and missionaries had discussed the overthrowing of the Hawaiian monarchy. Many businessmen wanted power. They wanted power to control labor laws and trade deals with America. They wanted progress. They wanted to bring more of the American ways to the islands. They waned to get rid of the traditional ways of Hawai'i they felt were slow and outdated.

Many missionaries wanted change because they were appalled by polytheism, the hula, and the promiscuity. The missionaries were also sugar farmers and wanted more profits. The Protestants wanted more churches on all of the Hawaiian Islands.

Just a few blocks from Waikiki Beach thirteen American businessmen secretly met in a private meeting room at their favorite restaurant. Even though most of the patrons were haoles, the topic to be discussed would be considered treasonous. They needed to act discretely and speak quietly. The main goals of the Committee of Thirteen were to overthrow the Hawaiian monarchy and create a republic ruled by these businessmen. They created the secret society known as *The Hawaiian League*.

Sanford Dole was the wealthiest and most powerful sugar farmer on the Hawaiian Islands. "Gentlemen. Please, please have a seat and let's begin the meeting." The other twelve businessmen sat with their whisky. "We have been complaining about the treatment and disrespect from King David for too long. It is obvious that negotiations do not advance our cause. Therefore we must look to other means."

Volney Ashford was the most vocal annexationist on the island, "Gentlemen, I must wholeheartedly agree with Mr. Dole! We have pleaded with King David and his sister to give us more freedoms. We asked for the right to bear arms. He denied us that right. We asked for more freedom to trade our sugar, pineapples, and coconuts across the Pacific. He denied us that as well. He denied us the ability to petition the United States government to become a territory. We will never become the enterprise we have dreamt of until King David is out of power. I can tell you that *The Riflemen* are ready. Nearly 200 of us have secretly trained to prepare to overthrow the king and his sister."

Lorrin Thurston, an American attorney jumped in, "I wish we could do this another way. I truly wish no harm to come to the king and his sister, but I have accepted the fact he will not give up the throne except by force. Therefore, with the blessing of most of you in this room, I have begun the process of creating the Hawaiian Constitution. We will have a constitutional monarchy like Great Britain. We will force the king to sign it, and then we can control the legislature to achieve all of our dreams and goals, and yes increase our profits!"

The thirteen men raised their glasses of whisky and yelled, "Hear! Hear!"

Dole spoke again, "It seems every time we get a new group of immigrant workers to accept our wages, they begin to unite against us or leave. The Chinese came in the 50's, and now many have left the fields to start their own businesses. Then the Japanese came in the 60's, and many have left for Kaua'i. Now the Portuguese have arrived by the thousands. All they want to do is start restaurants and make those damn malasadas!"

Thurston snapped back, "Have you had those malasadas? They are delicious!"

"Lorrin, you are missing the point. We can't keep them in the fields to maximize our profits!" Dole raised his voice.

Ashford joined in, "Yes please Lorrin. Let's be serious. We are about to start a civil war here and you're thinking about pastries!"

Sanford stood up, "I just got back from Haleiwa and Waialua. Those are our most productive fields. Farmers from both towns said they had to let acres of land go fallow because they couldn't get enough workers. They told me just last week three Japanese families moved to

Kaua'i and five of their Portuguese workers left to help the family restaurants. We need to do something fast! What is our next move?"

Lorrin raised his hand and cleared his throat, "Gentlemen, I have a solution. As soon as I finish the constitution I will sail back to Washington D.C. to start lobbying congress and President Cleveland to begin the annexation process. I believe the American sentiment currently is pro annexation of Puerto Rico, Cuba, and Hawai'i. All of these islands fulfill the demands for sugar and fruits to the American consumer. However, I will need funding, and a lot of it. I believe bringing the U.S. Marines to support *The Riflemen* will be all we will need to quickly stop any resistance the king might gather. I would say I could return by April."

Dole closed the meetings by commenting, "Gentlemen, I should remind you all before you go that America has trade competitors out there. Some might call them enemies. Great Britain and Japan would both love to control Hawai'i, its sugar trade, and Pearl Harbor. We can not let that happen!"

The Hawaiian waiter quietly entered and left the conference room on multiple occasions. He was smartly dressed with a white jacket and black slacks. They called him Johnny, but his Hawaiian name was Ka'ani Makoa. He was short compared to the American men. He was a handsome young man with his hair perfectly combed. He filled whisky and water glasses. He brought in the main dishes and cleared plates. He came and went just like the ocean breeze that blew through the open blinds of the restaurant windows.

The *Hawaiian League* was unaware that Johnny was spying on them. He was an assistant to Ambassador Baitmen. Johnny's boss's loyalty was to both King David and the country Ambassador Baitmen represented, Great Britain. He would ensure King David knew of the plans of the *Hawaiian League.*

After the meeting was over, Johnny told his boss he had an emergency and needed to leave. Johnny took off his jacket to blend in with the city people. He walked briskly in a meandering route to ensure no one followed him. He reached Ambassador Baitmen's residence and knocked on the door. It was late for visitors; nearly 8 PM.

Thomas opened the door slowly. It was difficult to see Johnny's face, but Thomas recognized him by his stature. "Johnny?"

"Yes, Ambassador. I have some troubling news. May I come in?"

Thomas opened the door wider, " Yes, of course."

Johnny looked back to the street one more time and walked in. "Ambassador Baitmen, the *Hawaiian League* is planning to overthrow the king. They have 200 armed men called *The Riflemen,* and plan to go to America to get the Marines to help."

"Did you hear anything about a timeline?"

"They are currently writing their own constitution and are planning on forcing King David to sign it to have a constitutional monarchy. Mr. Lorrin is planning on traveling to Washington D.C. to lobby the president and congress to annex Hawai'i!" They wish to be able to deploy this plan by April.

Keilani walked into the room, "What's all of the commotion my dear?"

"Johnny has brought us unsettling news. It appears that the *Hawaiian League* is planning a coup d'etat!"

Keilani questioned, "What's a koo detah?"

"They are planning to overthrow the king. They have 200 armed men and plan on encouraging America to annex Hawai'i my dear! This is horrible news. I must get to the king at once. Grace, can you please see if the telephone is working and call Lydia? We need to see them tonight."

Grace Keilani picked up one of Hawai'i's newest advances of western progress, "Hello operator?"

A voice on the other side greeted her with, "Aloha. How can I help you?"

"May I have Iolani Palace please? This is Ambassador Baitmen's wife; I need to speak with Princess Lydia." Grace patiently waited for someone at the palace to pick up.

A voice on the other end said, "Yes, she is here. One moment."

"Aloha. This is Lydia."

"Here you go ma'am," the operator said.

"Princess Lydia, this is Keilani. There is an emergency. Can we come over tonight to speak to you and King David?"

"Of course yes. Are you alright Keilani?" Lydia's voice was concerned.

"Yes, I am, but I believe you and the king are in danger. We will be right over. Aloha." They hung up the phone but the line was still active. The operator was Emily Thurston, the sister of Lorrin, and had been eavesdropping on the entire conversation.

Chapter 16
The Coup Begins
Manoa Valley, 5PM, January 11, 1887

Just a few miles north of Waikiki is Manoa Valley. The lush sloping mountains provide glorious views of the Pacific Ocean. On clear days a faint outline of Moloka'i can also be seen.

On most days rain comes from the northeast over Mt. Olympus and the Nu'uanu Cliff. Most of the rain pours on the steep slopes of Mt. Olympus and Nu'uanu Cliff. However, the rain often pushes over the ridge to feed Manoa and Waipuhia Falls. South a gentle mist casts rainbows so magnificent, they can be seen from Diamond Head to Western Honolulu.

The Hawaiians blessed by having residence up on the ridges surely felt the loving hands of the gods. The warm sunshine and gentle breezes made life near Manoa a true paradise. The missionaries, Buddhists, and businessmen who also had property in the elevated valley could watch from high above Honolulu as it slowly turned into a bustling city. From the higher elevation, these businessmen could see ships from much farther away than people near the shore. This allowed them to get to the docks to make the first negotiations for the shipments that came into the port.

Tonight, *the Hawaiian League* had other things besides business on their minds. Lorrin Thurston asked for an emergency meeting away from crowds and spies downtown. The Committee of Thirteen reconvened at Lorrin Thurston's luxurious mansion.

"Gentlemen, I asked you here, instead of in the city, because we have a spy amongst us. I received information last night that directly after our meeting, someone made haste over to the British ambassador's home. His wife made an emergency phone call to Princess Lydia warning her she was in danger. No one could have possibly known who wasn't in that room last night. I want to know if everyone in this room can swear to God their allegiance to our cause!"

All of the men began to talk at the same time in disbelief. Sanford Dole puffed on his cigar, exhaled, and said, "Gentlemen. I would like to be the first to testify on behalf of every man here. I have known you all many years and wholeheartedly believe it was none of us. I'd wager it was one of the restaurant staff. The busboys made their way in at times, and we didn't even notice what may have been overheard."

Volney Ashford agreed, "I concur with Mr. Dole. I trust every one of you with my life! I think it was one of those Hawaiian servants that were eavesdropping. I am concerned that the king will have time to plan to defend his palace when *The Riflemen* come to overthrow him."

Lorrin spoke up, "That was my fear. I think we need to change plans. As soon as I am done with the constitution, I will sail to America, but we cannot wait for congress and the US military to come help. I think we need to overthrow the king as soon as possible! Volney, when can your men be ready?"

Volney placed his half empty whisky glass on the table and thought for a moment, "If we are going to do this in complete secrecy, it may take a few weeks."

Sanford asked, "Lorrin, how much more time do you need to finish the constitution?"

"One week, but remember, we can amend it as we go. We will be in power. May I suggest we not delay. If the English or Japanese get involved, we could be in for a battle *The Riflemen* may not be prepared for. In all honesty, if this works out right, we can overthrow the king without firing a shot."

Sanford looked at the other twelve men, "Alright, how does this play out?"

Volney rolled out the map of O'ahu and placed four whisky glasses on each corner. "After we pick a date, I will travel to each village with volunteers and let our captains know. It will take me seven to ten days to get around the island. It'll take another four to five days for them to reach here. I'd say a couple more days to rehearse our plan. I'm thinking February 1st, we will be ready."

"What does 'ready' mean to you, Sir?" Sanford asked.

"I'll have nearly 200 well armed men. I'd think we leave here at 3 am. We surprise the king at his palace at the break of dawn with just a few sleepy guards to hold us back. Seeing how outnumbered they are, they will surrender. The first attack will be a wave of 100 men to assault the front of the palace. The other 100 will stay a block back. We will hope not to have to use them unless necessary. I would estimate it will take no more than ten minutes to get to surround the building so the king and princess cannot escape, have them sign the constitution by 9 am, and cook breakfast on the palace grounds."

Lorrin replied, "What if they have multiple armed guards? Will your men continue the fight? They are farmers, not soldiers."

Volney responded, "We have several men who served in the US military. Three of them fought in the Battle of Gettysburg! Captain Rupert Anderson fought in many successful battles for the South. His backbone is made of iron, and he is sly as a fox. They are experienced."

Sanford ended the planning with, "Then it is settled. We attack February 1. Godspeed gentlemen!"

Iolani Palace, Honolulu, January 11, 6PM

King David walked into his chamber to join his military advisors. A late evening thunderstorm was roaring over Honolulu. The loud explosions of the thunderclaps had everyone on edge. The emotions in the room appeared to be mimicked by *Kanehekili*, the Hawaiian god of thunder. Heavy gusts of winds slammed the palm trees against the lava rock of the palace. Intense down pouring of rain pelted the windows of the chamber. Lightning lit the room brighter than daylight, to be followed quickly by ear shattering thunder.

"Aloha. What an evening gentlemen!" King David walked over to his chair and began the meeting. "Please tell me where our training stands, Captain Melsun."

Captain Patrick Melsun was a fifteen-year veteran of jungle fighting in Indonesia. He realized the importance of guerilla tactics. "Your Majesty, we have been training for months. I believe we have 250 soldiers who are ready at a moment's notice to come to your aid. I can start moving the Howitzers and infantry into Honolulu in three days. I believe moving into the palace and strategic locations nearby need to happen under the cover of darkness. This way *The Riflemen* will not know that they are walking into a trap."

Captain Joseph Lewiston had served in the Navy and understood the power and impact artillery had on an enemy. "Your Majesty, I have the three Howitzers just blocks away. They are hidden and can be here in hours. My men have trained thoroughly. However, I must warn you that the anti-personnel shells will kill many men in close range. Your troops shoot accurately. I would suggest we move them here immediately. I would also build a structure to hide the cannons on the property. We will need shifts of men on duty all day and night. They might attack at any time. My feeling is once we fire a few rounds into them, they will retreat. However if all of their men come from all directions, a well-coordinated advance will overrun us. We will need all the men at the ready as soon as possible."

Captain Stephen Phipps had trained with the new Gatling gun. It was a hand cranked, but rapid-fire machine gun. "I believe the Gatling gun will be our 'ace in the hole'. We can place it on the roof. It is light and maneuverable. We can focus fire wherever there is a hole in the lines. If our men can get behind the lava rock walls, we will be well defended, Your Majesty. I also believe we immediately make another lava wall parallel to the gates where they will probably try to breach first. We should let them in easily. That way the ones on the outside won't know what is happening on the inside and they will keep coming into the trap."

Princess Lydia asked, "Do we know if they have cannons? Do we know their numbers? Or when they might attack?"

Captain Melsun stood, "Your Majesty, our intelligence shows they do have former soldiers from the Battle at Gettysburg. We have not seen any cannons. I believe they will attack from one front. That is what they know. I would wager however, it will be at night or early in the morning so darkness can cover their numbers. I would also wager that they will not wait for America's help. Our spies tell us they nearly have 200, and I'd wager they will be feeling confident with those 200 men. It will take them a couple of weeks to recruit all the men together. We should keep our spies on the lookout for movement of soldiers and men into the region."

Captain Leatherby then stood, "Your Majesty, I believe it would be prudent to assemble our troops quietly and as quickly as possible. We have established soldiers in hotel rooms at each corner around the palace. If I may, Sir?" He rolled out a map of the area, he placed decorative pieces of corral on each corner, "We have troops here, here, and here." He pointed to strategic upstairs corners of hotel rooms where soldiers could shoot *The Riflemen* from two directions.

King David shook his head, "Yes. This is a good plan. I think I must be seen on a regular basis near the palace so they continue with their attack. However, my sister must leave immediately and be protected around the clock by our guards. Until the storm blows over, Princess Lydia, I want you to go to stay at our Moloka'i home. You will be safe there. Chief Koka will assist us; I am sure of it."

Lydia looked sadly at Grace Keilani who was trying not to be seen in the back of the room.

Ambassador Baitmen raised his hand, "Pardon me, Your Majesty, I think it would behoove you to send me to Australia as soon as possible for more British armaments. I may not get back in time, but extra weapons and ammunition will be of help I am sure."

King David looked at Thomas, "That is a great idea. Please take *The Kamehameha* tomorrow. With any luck you can return before this begins. I approve of the plan gentlemen. Please travel safely out there, and get our troops here as soon as you can. We have several spare bedrooms and we can place the rest in those hotel rooms."

The meeting adjourned and the defenders of the kingdom left the king's chamber.

As the four captains stood in the storm on the porch they looked at each other. They lifted their collars towards the storm. Captain Melsun raised his voice to be heard over the wind," This is going to be a massacre. You know that right?"

Captains Phipps and Leatherby shook their heads in agreement.

Their boots splashed on the lava steps as they walked in silence towards the main gate. They walked just a block until they reached their favorite Ale House. Most of the patrons there were British. The captains only saw one drunk at the bar. The men sat down in a corner and ordered three pints of ale. They began to whisper to each other to coordinate their plans.

Chapter 17

Lydia and Moloka'i
Moloka'i, January 12, 1887

Princess Lydia stood on the bow of *The Kamehameha.* The princess took the advice of the king and fled to another island. The official news was for Lydia to vacation in Moloka'i for a time. King David had other plans.

The ship rose and fell gracefully as she cut through the waves. The ship was scheduled to land in Kaunakakai on the south side of Moloka'i, but the captain needed to land on Kalaupapa, the leper colony, to deliver emergency supplies. Lydia thought this would be a great opportunity to tour the village.

In the town square of Kalaupapa, the bell rang and rang. This was a sign for all of the villagers who could walk to make it to Main Street. An important visitor was coming!

Father Damien walked slowly through the neighborhoods yelling, "The princess is arriving! Look sharp!"

A crewman knocked on Lydia's cabin door. "Your Majesty, we are about to lower the boats."

Koa opened the door, "Queen Lydia will be right there." The crewman saw past Koa and saw the queen buttoning up her highest button on her collar. He glanced at Koa, smiled, and turned around.

"My Princess. Would you like me to come with you?"

Lydia adjusted her blouse, "I think this one I will do on my own. I don't expect any trouble." She looked in the mirror and fixed her hair a bit.

"As you wish, My Princess."

Three tiny dinghies manned with four men each rowed out to get the princess and other precious cargo. Today's haul was largely medical supplies. Unfortunately several villagers had been admitted to the emergency rooms of the hospital in the last week. The medical supplies would not save the patients, but would ease their suffering.

All the men on the rowboats were extremely nervous. Having the princess fall into the rough seas would be a disaster on many levels. Allowing the princess to get injured might end their funding and cause even more suffering among the villagers. It was the princess who convinced the king to fully support Kalaupapa with all medical supplies, food, clothing and building supplies.

Only through these weekly deliveries was the leper colony connected to the world. *The Honolulu Times* was always highly anticipated. Reading the newspaper allowed the villagers to feel connected to the world.

Lydia was unaware of the nervousness of the oarsmen. The princess climbed up the short ladder to the dock and was greeted by the hundred villagers that could walk down to the pier.

Father Damien placed a flower lei over Princess Lydia's head, "Aloha, My Princess. On behalf of all of us in Kalaupapa, we welcome you."

The crowd yelled "ALOOOO HA!"

Lydia waved and smiled, "Aloha to you. It is so nice to finally make it to..." A lepers face made Lydia freeze for a second, "Kalaupapa."

Father Damien asked, "How much time do you have, Princess Lydia? I would like to show you as much of our village as possible, but I am going slower in my old age."

"Our kind captain said I should leave well before dark to ensure my safe trip back to the boat."

Father Damien looked at his pocket watch, "Excellent! The sun will set behind these mountains in an hour. The mountains are so sheer we don't get to see the sunset in the winter. That leaves us with about two hours of light. May I escort you?" He waved his hand toward Main Street.

Lydia continued to wave as the villagers bowed and smiled, "How many people now live in the colony, Father?"

"Currently we have 142 souls here, Your Majesty. The number fluctuates weekly. Some pass away while others arrive. Our poor little cemetery is about to overflow. Many could not make it to greet you because they are either in the hospital or leprosy has destroyed their feet. It is a cruel and mysterious affliction. Some people have it on their faces as you have seen, while the rest of their body is perfectly normal. Some of us get it on our hands and feet, while our faces are perfectly normal. It's such a cruel, cruel disease."

The two were surrounded by the villagers who kept their distance. Lydia leaned in and asked quietly, "How contagious is it?"

"No need to fear," he said quietly, "It appears to be spread through saliva, usually the sharing of food. Plus no one will touch you, My Princess. Please do not fear us."

"You keep saying, us?" Lydia asked.

Father Damien looked away.

Lydia understood and said, "To be honest, Father, the ones with the sores on their faces are painful to look at. One took me by surprise on the dock."

"Oh it takes getting used to for sure." Father Damien changed the subject, "Here is our General Store." They walked slowly through the dusty door as a bell rang. "As you can see there is plenty of food on the shelves. I know you are the one who deserves the credit for making these afflicted souls' lives bearable."

Lydia leaned over to look at some of the canned foods, "I am so glad I can help."

The clerk shouted, "Aloha Princess Lydia. Is there anything I can get you?" He placed his mangled hand on the counter.

"Oh no Sir. I am fine! May I ask you a question?"

"Oh by all means, Your Majesty." The clerk replied.

"How is your quality of life here?"

"I'm not sure it could be any better, Your Majesty. To be honest, at first it felt a little like prison. I felt like I was trapped on O'ahu too, so I guess I just needed to pray. By God's grace, I, along with many others, have come to find this community as warm and loving as anything I could have ever imagined. The villagers are kind. Father Damien gives us spiritual and mental uplifting, and we have most of our needs met due to you. Mahalo, Your Majesty."

The couple left the store and walked through Main Street while enjoying a cool breeze.

"Give me just a moment, Princess, while I catch my breath."

"Are you alright Father?"

"I find myself having to catch my breath during long walks. Unfortunately it occurs more frequently these days."

At 3 o'clock the sun dipped behind the mountain. It began to sprinkle yet there were no clouds above.

Father Damien remarked, "Isn't this peculiar? These are rains from the other side of the mountains. They float a good mile or two before they bless our plants. I will say, My Princess, winters can be melancholy. We don't get to see the sunrises or sunsets. The sun dips behind the mountain early and it gets quite chilly at night here. The cool air comes off the ocean and brrrrr. It gets down into the 50s some nights."

"Oh dear, that is chilly. Father, what else can I do for the villagers here?"

"Oh My Princess, you have done so much. God provides what you do not." He smiled and looked upward. "Most people have gardens. Those healthy enough, pick coconuts, bananas, and papayas. We even have a small patch of sugar cane. We have a group of fishermen who bring in a small feast daily. However, medical supplies are always in need. Please keep them coming if you can."

"That is my intent, Father. Please feel free to ask for anything. I will try my best to serve my people. I especially feel the need to serve Hawai'i's wahines. I promise to do my best, Father."

Sheriff Wolo'ki walked up and bowed, "Aloha Princess Lydia. It is such a pleasure to have you here."

Lydia looked at Father Damien with curiosity and raised her eyebrow.

The Father looked back at the sheriff, " Oh, well yes. We do, on occasion, need the sheriff. But it is rare."

"Is there a jail here?" Lydia asked.

The sheriff waved the princess over. "Let me show you, Princess. It is off Main Street just a few feet. We placed it on the backside of Main Street so as not to upset any visitors or villagers. Most aren't even aware it is here."

Lydia looked inside and saw two cells. "Hmmm, interesting."

A young lady approached slowly and curtsied, almost falling over, "Forgive me, Your Majesty, for being late. My feet are in horrible shape and it took me a while to get here."

"Oh bless you for making your way to see me, Sister." Lydia smiled.

Father Damien opened his hand towards the visitor, "Princess Lydia, may I introduce to you Sister Dorothy?"

Lydia smiled and thought, "What an adorable little thing. What a shame she will never have a normal life."

Dorothy broke the silence, "I hope you enjoyed your visit." Lydia smiled again.

Father Damien looked at his watch, "Oh Your Majesty, we need to get you back to the ship. I hope you enjoyed your visit as well."

Only a few people were still following the princess. She waved aloha to Sister Dorothy and walked towards the pier.

"It was an amazing afternoon, Father. I hope to return again."

The sheriff escorted the princess and Father Damien back to the dock. "Please tell the villagers they are in my thoughts and prayers. I will keep the supplies coming. I promise."

Lydia climbed down the ladder onto the dinghy. As the small boat began to leave the pier, a large gust of wind blew Father Damien's vestment up slightly. His infected and mangled leg was exposed! Lydia turned her head quickly so not to let Father Damien notice that she had seen it.

The villagers came back out to the dock to wish the princess a loving "ALOHA!"

The princess looked back towards the dock. The men slowly rowed her back to *The*

Kamehameha. As the villagers on the dock got smaller, her sadness grew larger. The view tore her heart apart. Looking behind the people, Lydia could see the lush immense Kamakau Mountain. It gave Lydia joy that at least the lepers lived in one of the most beautiful places on earth. A small rainbow appeared to the east. To the west the orange glow of the setting sun highlighted the outline of the mountains.

"Was this paradise, or hell?" Lydia thought. Tears began to fall down her cheeks. She waved once again. Through many conversations with Kenneth Doel, her religious advisor, she would often ask him why the lepers had to go through this torture. She wondered, "God, why do you let your children suffer so?" Lydia was pleased that God allowed her to help ease their suffering.

Chapter 18
Chief Koka Apali of Moloka'i
Moloka'i, January 13,1887

Princess Lydia awoke from her nap. The anchor rattled the entire ship as it was lowered onto the rocks off the southern shore of Moloka'i. Lydia stretched, and sat up on her bed. A small candle lit the cabin. It was much shorter than she remembered when she laid down for her nap. She thought, "Well isn't that odd?" She yawned and stretched again. She decided to walk up to the deck to see if the moon was out.

As she walked up a ladder to the top deck she saw bright blue skies. The sun was just above the horizon. "I slept all night?" she thought.

"ALOHA Princess!" Captain Lathrop shouted. "I hope you slept well. The ocean was quite calm last night so I hope she did not rock too much."

"Oh Captain, I obviously slept like a log. What may I ask is on the agenda for today?"

The captain walked over to the princess. "Princess Lydia. I was trusted by our good King David to change the plans. Even you could not know."

"Oh really. Please tell me why our good king did not trust me with this information?"

"I believe the king said, and I quote, "You have the gift of gab.""

"HE DID NOT!" Lydia said indignantly.

"Please forgive me, Your Majesty, but he did. Our plans have changed so NO ONE will know where you are. The plan is to make a grand public entrance onto Moloka'i. Then in the middle of night, we are to sneak you off to Hulihee Palace in Kona on the Big Island. There, Queen Emma will hide you out for a few days."

"He trusts Queen Emma more than me? I must admit that does surprise me some."

"Your brother is quite a brilliant man. If the revolutionaries are looking for you, they will come here. However, you will be long gone and no one will know where you are. I will pick you up at night, and drop you off in Kona before sunrise. You have guards waiting for your arrival at the Hulihee Palace. From there, Queen Emma will take you to an even more secure place."

"Do my guards know about this plan?"

"I believe so, Your Majesty."

"Well, isn't he a smart one? Let's pray Queen Emma can be trusted and doesn't throw me into Manoa Loa to appease Pele." Lydia said with a smile.

A few dinghies rowed the princess and her guards to shore. As in Kalaupapa, hundreds of islanders lined the pier to greet the princess. The crowds shouted "Aloha", and covered her with flower leis.

Chief Koka Apali of Moloka'i greeted Lydia. "My beautiful princess! Words cannot express the joy the people of Moloka'i have for you and your visit. I understand you visited Kalaupapa yesterday. Your generosity fills our hearts for all of those poor souls afflicted with the leprosy. We too make the trek over the mountains to assist with their needs, but it is only homemade goods. I am sure you are weary from your journey. After you settle in at the royal summerhouse, please join me for our luau this evening. We have a special performance tonight and hope you will join us."

Lydia waved to the people, "Of course I will join you. Aloha everyone. I will see you tonight." A man caught Lydia's eye. He was tan and had a thin mustache and a patchy beard. He did not fit in and was not smiling. She nudged Koa to get his attention. Koa hissed at Sione. Sione noticed him too. The man turned and got lost in the crowd.

The princess arrived at the royal summer home. It looked as if it had been attended to on a daily basis. The palace had been dusted, the wood was waxed, the beds were made, and snacks and juice had been provided. The princess quietly asked her most trusted guard Koa, "Are you aware of what is to take place later tonight?"

He shook his head yes. "Everything will be taken care of, My Princess. Who do you think that strange man on the pier was?"

"I am not sure, but I got a really bad feeling about him. Please inform the other guards about him." Lydia looked around the room. She was looking for anything out of the ordinary. Lydia was rattled, but trusted Koa and her guards with her life.

As the winter sun began to set, a gentle sound of a conch blowing filled the air. It was time to join the luau. The princess and her guards, Koa, Sione, and Tafa, gathered in her carriage and slowly rode between the parade of admirers to the grove of palm trees where several tables and a small stage had been placed. Waiting was the chief of Moloka'i, his wife and several other dignitaries. They were all sitting at their tables eating their fruit and pupu platters. Lydia smiled and relaxed into the party atmosphere because she knew her guards were aware of the possible dangers.

A conch was sounded again starting the show. Men with torches and grass skirts ran around the perimeter and lit several tiki torches. The warm ocean breeze made all the tikis flicker, which lit the palm grove brightly. Looking back, the princess could see the palm tree trunks turn yellow from the light of the tikis. She could see hundreds of the villagers standing between the palms watching the show.

A village elder walked on stage. "Princess Lydia
Lili'oukalani, Chief Koka Apali, kanes, and wahines of Moloka'i, tonight we will share the history of Moloka'i."

Several drummers began beating a slow rhythmic melody. Several wahines in *Lole po'os*, and grass skirts began a slow sideways rising and falling of their hips. Lydia thought to her self, "these are the most graceful wahines I've ever seen!" She marveled about how beautiful her people were.

The speaker shouted, "The hula…" He lowered his voice, "…is soft. It is sweet. This lovely dance was first practiced right here in Moloka'i. Our beautiful wahines tell a story through dance. This is their interpretation of the gifts of Pele and Moana, *the ocean*. Centuries ago, the early Polynesians from the Marquesas Islands traveled in their canoes thousands of miles to reach Moloka'i." The drums picked up dramatically and the wahines ran off the stage as young kanes stomped and thrust their spears into imaginary foes.

The elder appeared to be angry, "War came to Moloka'i! Our ancestors had to fight to survive attacks from O'ahu and Maui! After many centuries, peace finally came to our island. Eventually we were all united by King Kamehameha the Great!."

The kanes kneeled as a man dressed in a huge yellow headdress walked onto the stage. "King Kamehameha united us into one Hawaiian nation! We hope and pray Princess, that you'll continue to protect us as our kings before you."

Princess Lydia smiled as the villagers cheered from behind the palm trees. As Lydia panned the crowd she noticed the suspicious man again. He was not cheering. He stood there motionless, staring. Lydia gave Koa a look and mouthed, "There he is again." Koa and Sione noticed him too. They moved his way, but the man once again disappeared, and this time into the darkness.

"We hope you will protect us like Kamehameha IV did. He created Kalapapau, and designated these ten acres of coconut trees to help feed us. He brought us cattle who have prospered on our western plains.

The princess replied, "I will do my best. However, King Kalakaua has many more years to reign. He teaches me every day how to be a good ruler."

The show went on for a while and then closed as all of the villagers sang *Aloha Oe*. This gave Princess Lydia great joy.

The crowd slowly dispersed and the princess and her entourage made their way safely to the summerhouse.

Lydia's third guard, Tafa leaned into the princess as she sat, "Princess, at midnight we will sneak down to the pier. We will keep the carriage and two guards from Moloka'i here to give the appearance that you are still here. Tavita will stand guard outside to reinforce the deception. That should be enough of a diversion to safely get you to the Big Island. IF anyone here is plotting to hurt you, they will be thrown off your trail."

Lydia sighed, "I am tired. Let me rest for a few hours and I will be ready at midnight."

At midnight, Sione lit his tiki torch and began his trip to the pier to see if it was safe. The streets were silent and no one could be seen. Taufa, Koa, and the princess crept a short distance behind. The moon was low on the horizon and appeared orange. It gently lit the streets, which allowed Princess Lydia to walk safely to the pier.

Men from *The Kamehameha* had already rowed to the pier. The surf was rather calm and the village was dark. Their getaway plan was working. There would be no reason to think the princess was not back at the summer palace. The crew and passengers inside the dinghy could not see much of the village at all. As the crew rowed out to sea, they could see the ship's light come into view and disappear between the swells. A billion stars were twinkling above. A small, but sudden wave tipped the boat to the left and Koa fell onto the princess.

"Your Majesty, a thousand apologies!"

It was almost pitch dark, but Lydia could see the outline of Koa's face. "Oh Koa… I am not harmed." Lydia closed her mouth and breathed in deeply. She could smell Koa clearly. She enjoyed it. Her mind was interrupted by sounds of the slaps of waves against the side of the boat, and an occasional splash of the oars on the water.

Chapter 19
Queen Emma and Princess Lydia
Moloka'i, January 14, 1887

A crowd had gathered around the summer
palace on Moloka'i to wish the princess a
morning aloha. Standing guard outside, Tavita

told the crowd, "The princess has become ill. She will be resting all day."

The crowd moaned with disappointment and slowly dispersed. Among them was the suspicious stranger.

The Kamehameha was already steaming past the south shore of Maui. The princess was on the top deck enjoying the breeze. For January, the weather was unusually calm and warm. To her left rose Haleakala, the massive dormant volcano that created the island of Maui. Molokini crater was off in the distance, and the much smaller island to her right was Lana'i. A pod of humpback whales was spraying just 100 yards from the ship. The joy the princess felt by the size and grace of those creatures made her even more grateful her brother made it illegal to hunt whales in Hawaiian waters. It was late morning as *the Kamehameha* sailed past Kalo'olawe. The plan was to pass any spying eyes of any neighboring islands and then wait in the Alenuihaha Channel until dark.

Soon after sunset, *the Kamehameha* sailed close enough to Kona to drop off the princess. A canoe rowed out to greet them. A man on the canoe yelled, "On behalf of Queen Emma, we welcome the princess! We are here to escort you to Hulihee Palace. The queen will meet you for breakfast tomorrow."

Lydia had never been on a canoe before. She was amazed at the timing of the rowers and the speed of the canoe. In just a few minutes the canoe slid upon the sand of Kona's bay. It was late in the evening. Like most towns in old Hawai'i, Kona was dark and quiet at night. The group slipped quietly into Hulihee Palace unnoticed.

January 15

In the morning, the roosters of Kona slowly awoke the sleepy town. Sione had stayed up for the night shift. He continued his patrol over to Tafa and Koa's room to get them ready for Queen Emma's visit. However, his first stop was at Lydia's room.

Sione knocked on Lydia's door, "Princess, Queen Emma is on her way."

There was a loud thump inside and Lydia replied, "Thank you, I will be right there."

Sione knocked again, "Is everything alright, My Princess?"

Lydia responded, "Oh yes. I will be right down."

Sione continued to watch the perimeter of the quaint little palace one last time. He ended up in the guards sleeping quarters. "Hey Lazy! Wake up!" Tafa mumbled something.

Sione yawned, "Hey where's Koa?"

Tafa turned over in bed, "Ummm, he told me he was going to make a security check around the palace."

"That's odd. I just checked the grounds and didn't see him."

Koa snuck down the hallway and tapped Sione on the shoulder, "The palace grounds are secure."

"I was just out there and didn't see you." Sione questioned.

Koa responded, "Weird. Hey Lazy, get up!"

Queen Emma was still thought of as royalty on the Big Island. After King Kamehameha IV passed, the people of the Big Island assumed Queen Emma would become queen of all of Hawai'i. However the constitution allowed the cabinet to pick the next heir and David Kalākaua had been chosen.

When her carriage rolled through town, the villagers came out to wave. Emma would visit Hulihee Palace on occasion so it wasn't that unusual for her to show up there. Sione was headed to sleeping quarters after getting himself some breakfast when Queen Emma appeared at the door, she stopped. She looked Sione up and down and said, "Hmmm. Where is the princess?"

Sione ignored the queen's flirting, and responded professionally, "Aloha, Your Majesty. She should be down stairs any moment."

Emma continued to stare, "Are you single?"

Sione was surprised by the question, "Ummm yes Your Highness. I am."

"I always did like the O'ahu men." She winked. Sione blushed.

Lydia's door opened, "Queen Emma! Aloha!" Lydia descended quickly down the stairs, curtsied, then strongly embraced the queen. The two walked arm in arm into the dining room to begin their breakfast and to catch up. The two had met on multiple occasions. It took some time for Queen Emma to come around to accepting King Kalākaua's reign, but she never held a grudge against Lydia.

Emma leaned in and looked Lydia in the eyes, "This is very important, Princess!" She looked left and right. Lydia became nervous. "I think I want to marry Sione," she giggled.

Lydia leaned back. "Oh you scared me, Emma. I thought something was wrong."

"Oh no. I'm serious. I've been a widow too long. I need a man in my life." She smiled.

Sione was trying to complete his last security check and both wahines looked his way and stopped talking. Then they looked at each other and laughed out loud.

"What?" Sione questioned. Questioning was out of protocol, but he knew what they were giggling about. He blushed again, turned, and headed out.

Sione passed Koa in the hallway, "Those two queens are like teenage girls. I'm going to bed." Koa replaced Sione in the dining room and stood guard.

Emma leaned into Lydia and whispered, "I'm serious. He's a gorgeous hunk of kane!"

"I'll put in a good word for you." Lydia winked at Emma.

"Now on a serious note, I believe you have another hideout for me."

Emma unrolled her map of the Big Island, "Let's look at this over here." She showed Lydia a remote village called Lapakahi. "It is not known by many people. They definitely keep to the traditional ways; it will be a refreshing change for you my dearest."

"I love it. It will get me closer to my roots."

Emma rolled up the map. "I think it's best that you go by boat. That way no one will see you. The people of Lapakahi have little contact with the rest of the world, except for an occasional fisherman or tradesmen. You will be living in a grass hut, eating fish, poi, and coconuts."

"Sounds…. interesting." Lydia said quietly.

The two royal highnesses chatted well into the morning like long lost sisters. "Perhaps I can take a nice carriage ride out to see you. How long will your dear brother expect you to live with us?"

Lydia shrugged her shoulders, "He said until the revolutionaries revealed their hand. I expect to be here for a few weeks."

Emma headed back down the hallway where Sione had just finished washing up after a long shift. She slid her pointer finger down his chest. "Come by my residence sometime would you? We can have dinner." Emma stepped in a little closer, stared at Sione for a few seconds, then turned and left.

Sione's face turned an uncharacteristic shade of red. Lydia was standing in the doorway of the dining room with a big smile on her face. "Perhaps we need to arrange dinner with you and Queen Emma upon our return."

"I would like that." Sione said with an awkward smile.

The plan worked perfectly. Lydia snuck out that night and arrived early at Lapakahi the next morning.

A royal canoe transported the princess and her guards. The 120 villagers of Lapakahi were as she was told. They all lived as Hawaiians had for centuries. They lived in grass roofed huts with the walls made of lava rock. All of the houses had windows that could be covered during the storms. There was no running water, no electricity, nor indoor bathrooms. When fresh water was carried into the village, the women helped each other shower by pouring the water over their heads to rinse out the crude soaps for which they traded fresh fish and jewelry. Most of the men were in the ocean daily and would occasionally use a sponge with fresh water brought by other villagers to reduce their body odor.

Fresh water was a luxury. Attempted aqueducts were crude and inefficient. When dry spells came, it was easier to just walk up the mountain to fetch a couple buckets each day. Water was needed for cooking, gardening, and showering. None was wasted.

The villagers spent their days productively. They fished. They cracked coconuts, and kukui nuts for oil. Some hiked up the golden hills to the taro fields to fetch water. These golden colored hills were foreign to Lydia. This was one of the driest areas of all of the Hawaiian Islands. The village stood on an elevated sand bank about ten feet above the ocean. Even during storms the waves did not flow over the raised shoreline. Sharp large lava rocks lined the shore. They had been left behind after an ancient lava flow. It served as a defensive measure the villagers had used to protect them selves more than once. Small paths to the ocean allowed the fishermen easy access to their small bay and manmade fishponds. Lava rocks had been placed out into the bay to create a barrier during low tide. During high tide, fish would swim into the ponds and be an easy catch for the experienced fishermen.

Looking across the channel, Maui could be seen through the ocean mist as Haleakala sloped gently into the clouds. It rarely rained or stormed here. The villagers were happy and busy. There was no crime and few arguments. Everyone contributed. Children were raised by all of the mothers. All of the villagers would come together an hour or so after sunrise. The men would meet and make a plan of where to fish, hunt, and who would get water, or work in the fields. The women made breakfast while discussing whose huts needed attention, who would tend to small gardens, or prepare the morning catch as the children played. Lydia, Sione, Koa, and Tafa joined in to share the responsibilities of four more mouths to feed.

At night, everyone got together for a huge communal feast. They told stories and sang. Lydia taught them Aloha Oe. The villagers accepted the special guest and her three guards like family, not having any idea who they were. They had never entertained guests like this. Rumors were swirling, but the new visitors kept their secret.

The guards were invited to stay in the bachelors' house. They joined three other kanes. They quickly became very good friends. The villagers were amazed that the guards weren't good at fishing or farming and teased them constantly.

Lydia was brought into an elder's house. They questioned her on a regular basis. Lydia was polite but diverted the topic. Lydia joined the chores of the wahines. Lydia felt like she belonged.

It was as if the princess had been sent back into time.

She would enjoy these few weeks more than any other time in her life.

Chapter 20
The Battle of Honolulu
The Streets of Honolulu, Feb. 1, 1887

The early morning showers had moved up into the Manoa Valley. A cool, early morning breeze began to blow. It was in the mid 60's, which is cool for Honolulu any time of the year.

The Minutemen quietly moved through the dark streets as they approached the king's palace. Nearly 200 men from around O'ahu were prepared to make history. Their requests had gone unanswered. Their frustrations had come to a boiling point. They felt that violence was the only way to pressure King Kalākaua to give in to all of their demands.

Captain Rubert Anderson and Captain Volney Ashford silently led the men down two streets for a frontal assault on the palace. Captain

Anderson's men would wait a block away for instructions after the gate was opened. Captain Ashford could not see over the ten-foot lava rock walls, and had learned in the Civil War not to commit all of one's troops until there was a clear opening and chance for victory. But Captain Ashford believed there would be little to no resistance. He was wrong.

King David gave all of his trust to the man who had saved his life a few months ago, Kenneth Doel. The only military experience Kenneth had was the leadership of a posse or two that rounded up escaped prisoners. However, Kenneth was sharp, he was loyal, and he worked closely with the British Commanders. He also knew many of *The Riflemen.* They were his neighbors and often revealed parts of the attack plan unwittingly to him. He had the king's soldiers prepared.

The king's gate was securely chained. It took Ashford's men over a minute to break the locks and chain. They were not quiet. This alerted Doel's security troops and gave them enough time to get to their positions. The British soldiers had trained the king's troops thoroughly on how to fire their rifles, their cannons, and the deadly new Gatling gun.

The king's guards shouted a warning, "STOP! or we will shoot!"

Ashford expected a few of his front men to get shot, but he sent them through the gate anyway. Fifty of *The Riflemen* were protected by the lava rock on both sides of the gate and could not see what they were getting into. It was very dark and the torches that lit the palace had been extinguished. The guards inside could see the men entering the palace, but the *Riflemen* could not see the royal guards.

The royal guards were instructed not to fire until men had entered the grounds. They did as they were trained. The first of two cannons erupted with thunderous explosions! The cannon balls ripped through several men, tearing their bodies to pieces. The guards begin to fire at close range at the silhouettes of men running through the gates. Then the Gatling gun began to fire. Ashford continued to send in men not realizing what was going on inside the gates.

Captain Anderson heard the cannon and Gatling gun. He looked at his Lieutenant Marez & Lewis, "Those aren't our guns! This is a trap! Let's go!" Lieutenant Marez and Lt. Lewis ordered the remaining 100 men to retreat.

A man on the other side of the gate peaked around the lava rock. "Captain Ashford! I can't see anything but our dead men. We need to stop!" Just then a soldier next to him was shot by a sniper, and then another. Ashford said this is a trap. They have snipers too.

Ashford held his men back. The shooting continued for a moment and then stopped completely. A voice could be heard in the distance, "Hold your fire!"

The screams of dying men and moans of the wounded could now be heard. *The Riflemen* still could not see inside the grounds. Ashford looked at his lieutenant, "We're not sending any more men in tonight."

Lieutenant Bradshaw screamed, "RETREAT!" The revolutionaries ran through the darkness of Honolulu for several blocks until they got to their horses. Half the horses were already gone. Captain Anderson's men had ridden off towards Diamond Head. Dawn's first light began to glow over the eastern Pacific. The streets were not quiet. Citizens opened their windows and peaked outside their doors asking their neighbors, "That wasn't thunder, those were gunshots right?"

Several horses were unclaimed. Each one was from a soldier that had been killed.

The guards lit their torches and started walking down the main walkway. The carnage was indescribable. Several men were still moaning and crying, pleading for help. The cannon balls turned several men into bloody masses of human remains. Other men had large holes in them from the Gatling gun. Others were wounded in the arm or leg and continued to beg for help. "Before we help these men, call the royal photographer down. We need evidence of this insurrection." Kenneth Doel said. "Koa, if you know of any doctors, please get them down here right away. We will also need transportation for the wounded to the nearest hospital. I want all the living to be arrested and handcuffed to their hospital beds."

Koa responded, "Right away, Sir!"

King Kalākaua was escorted by the British commanders to witness first hand the horrors of war. He vomited several times. "My God this is horrific!" he exclaimed as he covered his mouth with his handkerchief.

Kenneth replied, "Yes Your Majesty, it is. May I suggest we get to the Honolulu Times and make sure they run the truth about what happened here? A slanted story could bring the American military to their side, or even cause a declaration of war. We can't afford to allow the press to run lies about today."

The king soon realized Hawai'i, and his kingdom would be forever changed. He began to realize that the nickname of 'The Merrie Monarch' was about to change. "By the King's decree, I hereby proclaim that a royal observer must be present before any newspaper can be released." And just like that, freedom of the press was gone.

British Commander Leatherby spoke up, "Beg your pardon Your Majesty, but perhaps we should start the interrogations of all of our prisoners. That way we can arrest the leaders of this coup d'etat immediately before they strike again?"

"That is a great idea commander! I believe it is time we arrest these villains once and for all." And just like that, civil liberties were stripped as no arrest warrants were used, just the testimonies of the injured.

As the warming glow of the rising sunshine lit up the palace grounds, the death count began. All told 13 *Riflemen* were killed and 23 wounded. The king's guards had zero casualties.

An official royal observer rushed over to the plant where the Honolulu Times was about to run its first copy of the Battle Of Honolulu. The Headline read *"King's Troops Massacre Civilians"*. The royal observer stopped the presses. He added the photograph of revolutionaries on the palace grounds and testimonies of the wounded revealing that several American businessmen were behind the violent assault.

The new headline read, *"Violent Coup Thwarted by King's Guards!"*

The Battle of Honolulu would change the course of history for the Kingdom of Hawai'i, King Kalākaua, and his eventual heirs to the throne.

Chapter 21
Battle Aftermath
Honolulu, February 2, 1887

Honolulu was buzzing. Everyone was talking about the brief, yet horrible battle. Some talked of what they had seen. Some talked about who had been killed or wounded. Most of the people of Honolulu had no idea that a revolution had been brewing. Through conversations, they began to understand it was a small town and farmer issue, not a city issue.

King David called together his cabinet for an emergency meeting. Joining them were the three British commanders and his trusted friend, Kenneth Doel.

The king walked into the room and everyone stood. "Aloha everyone. Please be seated." King David was wearing his formal white jacket to express the urgency of the matter. "I have a few things I need accomplished today. I'd like Commander Leatherby to give his opinion on how to prevent this from happening again."

Commander Leatherby stood up and with a strong British accent, "In my experience, matters like these have happened in South Africa and India. We need to chop off the head of the snake! We just stepped on the tail, but the snake will still be angry. I propose we keep all the wounded in jail and try them for treason, which could mean the death penalty. We reduce their sentences if they cooperate. We can use their testimonies to arrest the leaders. I would pressure them with a plea deal in exchange for all the leaders. If not, a life sentence for treason would be more appropriate than the death penalty. Hard labor in their own fields might be an extra incentive for further revolutionaries not to do such things. I would also suggest we take the leaders' farms and sell them in multiple units. This will prevent the leaders, or anyone else, from having power in the future. We might consider expelling some of the leaders from Hawai'i indefinitely. I hand off to Commander Mulsen to discuss the information we do have."

Commander Mulsen stood up. He was a stocky fellow. He was only five foot four, broad, and strong as a mule. "We have the names of several leaders. We should invite the press to be there to take photographs. These front page photographs will pressure all future revolutionaries to go back to their farms and drop this insanity." He looked at the king for confirmation.

King David nodded his head. "This must end today!"

"Very good, Your Majesty. After we are finished here, I will take a large police force with me to arrest those traitors. They include; Rubert Anderson, Josiah Lewis, Franklin Marez, and Volney Ashford. I will have to wait until tomorrow to arrest Anderson and Ashford because they are in Haleiwa."

King David was surprised Sanford Dole's name was not on the list.

Kenneth Doel shook his head, "I know some of those men."

King David, "I would like for you, Kenneth, to be there and report back to me as soon as possible. Perhaps we should impose martial law. No one on the streets after dark until further notice."

Commander Leatherby spoke up, "Beg your pardon Sir, but is it wise to punish the people of Honolulu? It appears these rebels are all from the countryside."

"Thank you for your concern, Commander, but for the safety of the people, we must keep the streets quiet, at least for a few nights."

February 3 – Haleiwa

Rubert Anderson was working in his field. The sugar cane in this part of his farm nearly reached his eye level. A Portuguese farmhand pointed to a man riding quickly up Anderson's red dusty road. Rubert could clearly see the rider on top of the horse. Rubert took off his hat and fanned himself. The rider continued at full speed and forced the horse to brake hard, kicking up a dust cloud.

Before the dust could settle, "THE BRITISH ARE COMING!" Ashford screamed!

Rubert leaned on his shovel, "You're kidding me right?"

Ashford got off his horse and rushed up to Rubert, " I am not. Some British blokes with the police and the military are rounding up and arresting the men who were at the massacre. Josiah and Franklin have been arrested, and I hear they are coming for us!"

Rubert looked up at Ashford, "Where are they now?

"A few miles outside of Pearl Harbor. They are on horseback, but moving slowly. I figure you have a couple hours, Rubert."

"Well we knew this could happen. I knew we should have surrounded the palace when we attacked. Damn it! I'd better get Tracy to pack up and get us out of here. Are any ships leaving Haleiwa today, Ashford?"

"Yes. Our weekly shipments leave today at noon. You have about three hours if you plan on making it. I know I will be on it. I'm not going to prison. I'll go back home to Sacramento."

"Ashford, what about your farm?"

"Hell, it hasn't been that profitable lately anyway. I just got paid from my last sugar shipment. I'm going to run to the bank to get all of my savings and get on that ship. I suggest you come with me."

Ashford jumped back on his horse and rode quickly back into town. Rubert ran back to his house. The farm worker turned around. He headed towards another group of Portuguese workers to spread the news.

When Rubert reached his house, he instructed Tracy to pack whatever she could carry. "What should I pack? Where are we going? What's going on Rubert?"

"Sweetheart, the military is coming to arrest me! We have to go to the pier now and take the noon ship to California!"

"Oh my God, Rubert! I knew this rebellion thing was a horrible idea. I've never been off O'ahu! I've never even been on a ship! This is crazy!"

Rubert walked over to Tracy and grabbed her shoulders, "Listen Honey, I am not going to prison, and they will probably put you in prison too. They will assume you were in on it. We can go to the bank and clear out my account. That will be plenty of money to give us a start back in California!"

In 20 minutes, the couple was packed and ready as they rode in their carriage to Haleiwa. They left most of their belongings in their modest farmhouse. Rubert cleaned out his bank account, and they made it to the ship where Ashford and his wife were waiting. At noon, the ship began to slowly move off the pier. Tracy was petrified. The ship was loaded with sugar for California. By 12:15 the cargo ship had turned and was headed full speed towards California.

Ashford motioned for Rubert's attention, "Come to the stern and look at the pier."

Rubert and Tracy made their way to the back of the ship. They could see the commotion of several police and the military on the pier. They had barely escaped justice. Rubert and Ashford hugged. Then they noticed some of their workers on the pier pointing.

Ashford looked at Rubert, "Look at those ingrates! They ratted us out. How else would the military know where we were?"

"Well Ashford, that doesn't matter now. We have enough cash to start a new life in California. Where are you going to go?" Feeling safe and relieved, the insurrectionists began to plan their futures.

Ashford gazed back at the pier as the military turned around, "My parents and brother still have a nice sized farm outside of Elk Grove California; it's about twenty miles south of Sacramento. There are only 25 farmers there, but they have a restaurant and hotel. The railroad comes by once a day to bring supplies. How about you?"

Rubert put his arm around Tracy, "I'm from Antelope, California. It's about twenty miles north of Sacramento. The PFE, I mean the Pacific Fruit Exchange, rolls right through the community. There's no hotel, but the community does have a little school called Center Elementary. We hope to have plenty of children one day. This $500 is all we have, but that will definitely get us started. We will have to get together some day. Heck, we could catch the PFE, transfer at the rail yard, then catch the Union Pacific down to Elk Grove. We could be there in a couple hours."

"My mom loves visitors and makes the best pumpkin pie." Ashford remembered a letter his brother had written to him a few months back. "Hey Rubert. My brother tells me there are quite a few sugar beet farms in the Sacramento Delta area. Perhaps we can get down there to see if we can start a sugar farm again. What do you say?"

Tracy looked at Rubert with a smile. "I think we should give it a look. Does the ship always move like this?"

Chapter 22
A BIG Reunion
The Big Island, February 4, 1887

King David arranged a meeting between himself and Queen Emma. It was clearly time that he and Emma mended fences. While on the Big Island, he would pick up his sister from Emma's secret hiding place.

As King David set foot in Kona, his head was flooded with emotions. In the Kona-Kailua area, most of the villagers had remained loyal to Queen Emma, as she was once wife of Kamehameha IV. Queen Emma, along with many of her subjects, felt she was the rightful ruler of all of the Hawaiian Islands, not just the

Big Island. However, the greeting was polite and cheery.

Queen Emma strolled along the beach and curtsied to her king. This was a big step in improving relations with King David. Having the villagers of Kona see this respect helped to improve the mood of the reunion. The two embraced and she led King David on a short stroll along the bay to Hulihee Palace where they were to dine. Hundreds of villagers came to witness history. It was the first time King David Kalākaua had set foot in Kona. Seeing the old and new royalty together gave a feeling that Hawai'i would remain a kingdom for years to come. Word had already reached Kona regarding King David's bravery in repelling the rebels. Along the way to the palace, many villagers congratulated King David on his achievement. David was full of joy.

The pair of royals entered Hulihee Palace. Queen Emma said, "Please come to the dinner table. We have quite a feast for you. We also have room for your British commanders and the Baitmens. We've heard your British commanders were extremely brave defending your palace."

Commander Leatherby responded, "Your Majesty, you are too thoughtful. Thank you for your hospitality. I am famished."

Thomas and Keilani also thanked the queen. The Baitmens were allowed to spend the evening with Queen Emma.

Emma looked at Keilani, I understand you and the princess are quite close?"

Grace Keilani answered, "Oh I adore her. When we are not traveling to Australia, I enjoy spending as much time as possible with her."

"What is Australia like Keilani?" The queen wondered aloud.

"They have the most unusual creatures there. At their zoo, we saw a creature called a platypus. It has hair and looks like a mongoose, but has a bill like a duck. We also saw what looks like a giant deer but jumps on its hind two legs. It is called a kangaroo!" Her excitement grew. "Plus they have this creature that looks like a dinosaur. It's called a crocodile. It is green and has thick skin with a mouth two feet long and has a massive tail. It must have been ten feet long!"

Emma looked at Keilani as if she was crazy, "Oooookay."

Thomas spoke, "Your Majesty, she does not exaggerate. These animals are bizarre!

The party all sat together. The dinner consisted of piping hot pork that had just been removed from an underground pit, guavas, pineapple, coconuts, newly arrived grapes, and fresh mahimahi. A servant filled up everyone's glasses with rum from Kaua'i, "Cheers! Long Live the king!" Emma stated with exuberance.

All the diners cheered and began to eat.

After most of the idle chit-chat and eating had been completed, the king spoke. "Queen Emma, I am so thoroughly pleased we can finally get together. It has been too long. I believe we have extinguished the rebels and their cause on my island. The whole ordeal made me realize that it may happen to you … and to the chiefs on other islands."

The queen spoke, "We are doing our best to remain in good standing with our ranchers and coffee growers."

"Well that is good news. I have thought a lot about how to proceed with the rebels. A few of the rebels have left O'ahu, and we have punished the leadership. However, I am trying to open lines of communication with the other rebel farmers that participated in the coup attempt to improve their lives, as well as ours. The honest truth is, we need the farmers to bring income and jobs to all of the Hawaiian Islands. I want to reach an agreement with them so everyone benefits."

Emma cleared her throat, "I wholeheartedly agree. The villagers struggle with how quickly things are changing. They worry that our beautiful culture will end. And yet, they love the new foods and machines that make their lives easier. Have you seen the newest can opener? It is simply amazing! It seems that when every new ship that comes in, a new wonderful invention comes to us."

"It is on the minds of all of the Hawaiians. The new railroad in Maui is simply unbelievable. This loud monstrous contraption can do the work of one hundred men. We are more efficient, yet it puts workers out of jobs. I am quite conflicted," David said sadly.

"These are amazing times." The queen looked at her guests.

"Queen Emma, the real reason I am here is to make sure Hawai'i can be controlled by Hawaiians. I want us to be able to work together so we may control our own destiny. If we are united, we are much less vulnerable to attacks. I am asking for your support and loyalty. May I have it?"

"Your Majesty, I am PROUD to serve you and the Hawaiian people. You have my complete loyalty. I will always be Queen Emma and serve and lead my people here on the Big Island, but you are the king of all of the Hawaiian Islands."

David smiled, "That fills my heart with faith and joy. Please let me know how I can serve the people of the Big Island." David changed the subject, "Now that we have that settled, I am curious. Where is my sister?"

Emma's face lit up, "Oh I can't wait to take you there! She is in a small, unknown village on the north shore called Lapakahi. They rarely see other Hawaiians or haoles. She has her three bodyguards with her: Koa, Tafa, and Sione. One, who I must say I want to see again."

David laughed out loud, "Emma! You have fallen for one of the guards? Let me guess, Sione?"

"As a matter of fact, it is Sione. I have been a widow for many years now, and I think he'd be an amazing companion for me." Emma reached for her fan.

"Well, well, well. We will have to give Sione some time off. Perhaps a long vacation here in Kona."

Emma blushed as she fanned herself, "That would be lovely. We leave for Lapakahi in the morning. I thought we would take a few carriages with extra supplies as a thank you to the villagers of Lapakahi for protecting her. It is about a four-hour ride. Some of the road has been covered by older lava flow, which slows down the carriage. Pele and Mauna Loa have been busy.

"I can not wait. I miss my sister."

February 5

It was nearly noon when the group arrived on the north shore of the Big Island. The bumpy road began to wear on the patience of Emma, David, and their guests.

A man on the top of the hill started blowing into a conch. King David was unaware of the activity behind the hill. Down in Lapakahi, that conch sound meant a special guest was coming. The villagers quickly dressed more appropriately. Nudity was common in the village, especially on hot days. Lydia walked out of her hut to see what the commotion was all about. "What is going on Cousin?"

"Oh, a special guest is almost here! We like to look our best."

The conch sounded again and multiple carriages and men on horses could be seen. The guard at the top of the hill asked the carriages to wait.

All of the villagers gathered to sing the welcome song to the king and queen of Hawai'i. Both Emma and David stood at attention while the villagers sang their welcome song. Lydia finally recognized her brother and she began to run up the hill. David carefully stepped down the hill as the trail had been made with sharp lava rocks. As the two embraced, they both said, "I have so much to tell you."

Queen Emma walked down and Lydia laughed, "Oh my goodness what a special surprise! There is so much I need to share with you." Lydia looked behind Emma and there was Keilani. "Oh my goodness; it keeps getting better and better."

Lydia and Keilani embraced, looked at each other, and embraced again. "Oh, my Keilani. My heart is filled with such joy right now!" Lydia, locked elbows with Keilani and then with Emma. The three giddy girls walked down the stony path to the village. They passed right by David as he stood with his arms crossed, shaking his head.

"Wow!" The king said. "Now I know where I rank." He laughed as the wahines strutted by him.

Thomas made his way down to the king, patted him on the shoulder and said," Women, Your Majesty, they are quite the mystery."

"Indeed, Thomas, Indeed."

Lydia yelled to her new family, "Cousins, may I introduce to you Queen Emma of the Big Island!"

The villagers yelled "Aloha!" and bowed.

"This is my dear friend Keilani from O'ahu."

"Aloha Keilani."

"And this amazing man is King David Kalākaua, king of all the Hawaiian Islands!"

The villagers had never met royalty before. They all went to their knees. David walked up to Lydia and quietly asked, "What should I say?"

"You are the king. Say something… kingly," she said with a smile.

David cleared his throat, "Dear people of Lapakahi, please stand. On behalf of myself, Queen Emma, and all the Hawaiian people, I want to thank you for protecting my sister and heir to the Hawaiian throne, Princess Lydia Lili'oukalani." David applauded them.

A few of the villagers looked at each other and whispered, "Lydia is our princess?"

Some of the friends Lydia had made ran up to her then abruptly stopped, "May we hug you?"

"Of course you can." Lydia proceeded to hug many of the village wahines.

Emma continued down the steps into the village waving to the villagers until she came upon Sione. Her heart raced. "Aloha Sione."

"Aloha Queen Emma. It is so nice to see you again."

Emma started to blush, "I was hopeful you could take me around the village as my tour guide."

Sione glanced over at Tafa. Emma looked back at Lydia and they were both smiling. Sione waved his hand as if opening a door, "This way please. Oh look, my Queen! Humpback whales are breaching in the distance.

Tafa gave Sione an approving nod and a wink. Koa was thinking to himself, "I'm actually a little jealous."

For most of the afternoon, the conversation went back and forth between Lydia, David, and Keilani. Thomas sat quietly and politely listened to their adventures. Lydia and the guards all had so many special events happen to them. The entire group of visitors made merry for King David. After so many days of worry, David felt like he was the Merrie Monarch once more. The villagers were worried their village was not suitable for a king and a queen, but decided it was good enough for a princess, and they slept just fine that night.

The next morning was bittersweet. Lydia told the villagers it was one of the best times of her life. She hoped they would accept the gifts the king and queen had brought them. The king brought extra blankets, medicine, and food. Lydia cried as she hugged and said aloha and mahalo to her new cousins.

Koa, Tafa, and Sione hugged and slapped the backs of many of the kanes who had become great friends.

"I promise to be back soon." Lydia knew she would keep her promise. The royal group began the slow trek back to Kona. Keilani put her arm around Lydia in the carriage as Lydia wept.

David and Thomas joined the two ladies. Queen Emma was about to ride by herself until she yelled out, "Sione, are you not going to join me?"

Sione looked at Tafa who was on horseback with him, "I got your horse, Cousin'. Go enjoy yourself." Sione smiled at Koa.

Lydia looked back one last time. "Oh what a magical place Lapakahi is, Keilani. The people are so… beautiful. I felt like I was transported back to old Hawai'i. I have to be honest, I think I like the old days better. Maybe progress isn't such a good thing after all."

Chapter 23
The Economy Crumbles
Kings Palace, Honolulu, June 1890

A few years had passed since the Battle of Honolulu. Talks of rebellion had gone quiet after *The Hawaiian League* was disbanded and imprisoned.

However King David had made a miscalculation on the impact of so many Americans being forced to close their farms.

Sugar and pineapple production dropped significantly. California buyers and consumers grew impatient with the lack of consistent production from the islands and had begun to shop with Central American countries.

Tax revenues decreased. Unemployment increased. King David needed sound advice from those skilled in international business. He called forth his cabinet.

"Ladies and gentlemen, please have a seat." Eleven of King Kalākaua's most trusted allies sat down and scooted in their chairs. Among the cabinet were Thomas Baitmen, his Chief Ambassador; Kenneth Doel, his Chief of Staff; Commander Leatherby, his Chief of the Military; Commander Lewiston, Commander of the Hawaiian Navy; Commander Pat Melsun, Chief Foreign Military Ambassador; Chief Kaanapali of Maui; Chief Koka Apali of Moloka'i; Chief Peke of Kaua'i; Taufa Tupu Head of Security; Queen Emma of Hawai'i, Sione Tupu, Personal Body Guard of Queen Emma, and Princess Lydia.

King David opened the meeting, "I would like to welcome our newest member, Sione Tupu. He is the personal bodyguard of Queen

Emma and commander of the Big Island Military."

Taufa leaned over to Chief Kaanapali and whispered, "I bet he's guarding her body alright."

Chief Kaanapali laughed out loud and attempted to turn it into a cough.

"Are you alright, Chief?" King David asked. The chief just grabbed a handkerchief and covered his mouth and waved as if to say he was fine, then elbowed Taufa.

"I called the cabinet together to address our struggling economy. Sugar and pineapple production has dropped over 30% this year from last, and this year's crops looks like it will be even worse. Add to that the growing cost of our military has skyrocketed. Kalapapau is becoming more expensive, and with the growing attendance in our school system, the costs are at an all time high. At this rate I will not be known as the 'Merrie Monarch', I will be known as the 'Bankrupt Monarch'. I need this group to find a way to help this economy rebound. The exact figures are on the document in front of you.

Commander Leatherby raised his hand. "Yes, Commander," said the king.

"We can easily train less, Your Majesty. We could reduce the amount of ammunition used for practice, and we could move most of the troops to reservists. However, to do so would jeopardize our readiness."

"Thank you. I understand your concern and those cuts will help. I believe the excessive training will have to be sacrificed for now. Anyone else?"

Kenneth raised his hand, "Your Majesty, perhaps a goodwill tour to California will increase business interest again in Hawai'i. We could begin the talks of our plan to make that merger between California and Hawai'i sugar, C & H. I think that would be one great way to increase the influx of foreign money and increase tourism. With the newest luxury liners, visitors can get here in days from San Francisco, Los Angeles, and Seattle. A couple hotels in the Waikiki area could bring thousands of dollars to Hawai'i. Plus if we could convince travelers from Asia going to America, and vice versa, to stop here for some

R & R like the navy does, we could really reduce unemployment here in Honolulu. Think of the number of jobs that could be created."

"Kenneth, those are amazing ideas! By the way everyone, congratulations to Kenneth, he is about to become a father for the first time." The cabinet applauded.

Unbeknownst to the group, there was another expecting father in their midst.

"Ahh thank you. My work is done." He smiled, "Now it's up to my dear Mary to do her part."

Lydia asked, "Have you picked out a name yet?"

"Well if it's a boy his name will be David Kenneth, in honor of Your Majesty." David smiled. "If it is a girl, she will be named Elizabeth Lily, after the princess."

Lydia sighed, "That's the sweetest thing, Kenneth. I am honored because I am sure it will be a beautiful girl. Besides, boys are smelly." Lydia teased.

Some of the cabinet members jokingly sniffed their armpits.

King David looked at Lydia with a scolding glare, like older brothers do sometimes when scolding their younger siblings.

"Sorry, Your Majesty." Lydia said softly, after being scolded.

David snapped to get everyone back on track, "Anyone else with a business idea?"

Queen Emma spoke up, "Your Majesty, a group of scientists were on the Big Island the other day doing research on Mauna Loa and Mauna Kea. They called themselves volcanologists, I think. We had the oddest conversation. They want to compare our volcanoes to Chief Kaanapali's Haleakala. I believe they said ours are active and Haleakala was dormant, or sleeping. They would like to set up a small outreach campus from Stanford. They said they could help build it, and of course would pay us for the land."

The king thought for a moment, "Does anyone know how common active volcanoes are? Because if they are not common, I bet we could get scientists from around the world to come and study, and of course pay us to do so."

Queen Emma replied, "That's what I was thinking. They also said they expect Haleakala to blow up like Diamond Head one day!"

Chief Kaanapali's eyes widened with fear, "Do these scientists know when?"

Emma teased, "It could be this year." She waited, "Or it could be a thousand years from now." She teased again, "They also said our Mauna Loa wouldn't blow up for at least ten thousand years!"

Chief Kaanapali just grunted, "Hmmmm." The chief did not seem to like the response.

David said, "Let's start promoting this to Stanford."

Thomas spoke up, "Your Majesty, may I suggest that if you were to tour California, perhaps include a tour to Stanford University to speak to these scientists. I am sure the press would have you on the front page. I also know a few professors from the University of

California, Berkeley. They would not look favorably on Stanford getting an advantage over them. I would wager they would also like to do a joint sister school with Hawai'i. The two universities are a day's ride apart."

Princess Lydia politely, but out of protocol, called David, "'Brother, I beg of you, PLEASE do not cut funding to Kalaupapa. I made a promise to Father Damien I would do everything in my power to keep the suffering of the lepers to a minimum. Life has already been too cruel to those good people. Please do not make their lives more difficult. If I have to, I will go door to door to raise money for them."

David paused and clasped his hands together, "My dear cabinet, there are two groups of people I do not want to harm in any way. The first is the children of Hawai'i. So we will do whatever is necessary to educate them. The second are the sick. Do not worry, Princess. We will continue our shipments to Kalaupapa." Lydia smiled and breathed a sigh of relief.

"Excellent ideas everyone. So it appears I am going to California!"

Chapter 24
San Francisco
San Francisco Bay, September 10, 1891

Mark Twain was quoted, "The coldest winter I ever spent was a summer in San Francisco." The frigid waters of the Northern Pacific fill the bay creating fog banks and bitter cold winds.

King David debated for days on what to wear as his ship, *The Kamehameha,* steamed into San Francisco Bay. Keilani was five months pregnant and was treated more like royalty than King David. She suggested, as the ship got close to the bay, the king should look royal and Polynesian. His bright yellow regalia with bright green leaves truly gave him an air of royalty.

What the king did not account for were the bay breezes. Even though the sun was shining, the king could feel the bite of the ocean wind. King David looked to Keilani, "I have never felt such cold air. Look at my goose bumps!"

"My apologies, Your Majesty, I should have known you would not be accustomed to the cold breezes here. However, I must say you look magnificent!"

"Thank you my dear. Coming from you, my sister's dearest friend, that means a lot." David waved to the thousands of people that came out to greet the King of Hawai'i.

From the bow they could see a small island in the middle of the bay with a concrete structure at the top of a hill. "Captain Dale, what is that building there?" David asked.

Captain Dale Lathrop turned his head to the port side, "Oh that is Alcatraz Prison. It used to be a lighthouse, then an outpost during the Civil War, and then the government turned it into a prison. They say it's impossible to escape from. These waters are cold and rapidly moving. No one can swim to shore even if they busted out."

"Perhaps we could make a prison on Kaho'olawe?" The king looked at Thomas.

"You know sir, that sounds expensive. You are right. It would be impossible for people to swim to Maui with all the sharks and jellyfish. I have also heard that some countries ship their prisoners to other countries, and pay to do so. Great Britain has done that with Australia."

The king thought for a moment of the logistics of that, but his thought was interrupted when *The Kamehameha* blew its horn and the crowd waved and cheered. It would take a couple of hours for the tugboats to position the king's ship to its mooring. After standing out in the cold air for some time, King David decided to go below to his quarters to change into his more western, and warmer, royal garb.

As he walked down the plank to the dock, photographers and politicians lined up for a formal greeting. Governor Henry Markham introduced himself, "Welcome to California, Your Majesty! We are so excited that you are honoring us with your visit; we have so much planned for you!"

"I am so grateful. I have heard so many wonderful things about California and would like to see as much as I can in the next few weeks."

"I would like to introduce to you the mayor of this great city, Mayor Edward Pond."

"Aloha Mayor Pond. I would like to give the two of you these gift baskets." The baskets of gifts were so heavy, they could barely be carried by one person. Inside were a beautiful assortment of live hibiscus, elephant eared vines, pineapples, coconuts, bananas, and coffee. "All of these are grown on our beautiful islands," David boasted.

Mayor Pond replied, "Oh dear! I have never seen such beautiful flowers. I am hopeful you can join the governor and me for dinner and a show. We have arranged for your dancers to perform tonight as well."

"Oh they call me the Merrie Monarch for a reason, Mr. Mayor. I love to celebrate!"

Governor Markham asked, "What shall we call you?"

"Kalākua might be difficult to say, so how about King David?"

Governor Markham, " I must say King David, your English is superb!"

"I was tutored from a young age in the Queen's English. I hope my accent is not too strong?"

"Oh my no. I think it is quite charming, Your Majesty." Markham smiled. "Oh and here is the businessman I would like to introduce you to. His name is Walter Blake. He represents several sugar beet farmers and currently the California Sugar Company."

"Aloha! Mr. Blake! Oh yes, we have met before." The king winked.

"Aloha?" He said shyly with a smile.

"That was wonderful. To all of you here today, ALOOOO HA!" David yelled joyfully.

The crowd cheered again and the press took multiple pictures as the dignitaries waved to the onlookers on the way to their carriage.

Mayor Pond spoke again, "Oh I almost forgot, here are two Deans of Volcanology I would like you to meet. This is Dr. Nicholas Low, from Stanford University, and his brother Dr. Christopher Low from University of California at Berkeley."

"Aloha doctors. Your parents must be so proud to have two doctors in the family."

Dr. Nicholas replied, "Oh indeed they are. We are quite excited about the opportunity to study your Mauna Loa and Mauna Kea volcanoes. Have you spoken with Queen Emma?"

David winked, "Well, I will need to get Pele's permission, not Queen Emma's. I am sure with the proper tribute, both of those strong wahines will allow it."

Dr. Christopher asked, "Who is Pele, Your Majesty?"

"Oh, she is the goddess of the volcanoes. You do NOT want to get her angry! Trust me, that wahine has quite the temper! Once I was on a whaling vessel not far from Kona, and Pele got so mad she exploded. Rocks from twenty miles away landed so close they almost sank our ship!" David's face became animated.

Nicholas responded, "Oh My! Well we will certainly give her due respect, Your Majesty. We want to respect your culture. Oh, here are my daughters, Kory Lynn, Kally Lou, and Alysha May. They are following their father's footsteps and will be traveling to

Hawai'i with us. They are all single." He smiled at the king.

Kory Lynn tapped her father on the shoulder with her fan. "Oh Daddy."

David smiled, "It just so happens that there are several single men on board, and too many to count on the Big Island."

Governor Markham interrupted, "I hope you are comfortable with a large police force. It is not often we have royalty. We want you to feel comfortable, and be safe. Not that we expect any trouble. Why don't you let the Mayor's staff take care of your entourage, so you and Ambassador Baitmen can join us in our carriage."

David peaked out of the window, "Your buildings are incredible. They are so tall. We have nothing like this in Hawai'i."

Mayor Pond boasted, "The growth is unbelievable. We are having to deal with growth like most American cities. Houses, businesses, and apartments seem to go up every day. When you add sanitation issues, crime, medical issues, and schools, it can be quite strenuous running a city."

King David sighed, "Oh I know how difficult it can be. Since you brought up the subject of progress, Mayor, Hawai'i truly wants to improve business relations with California - and America, of course. Ever since the coup attempt, our sugar and pineapple production has dropped. Our import tax revenues are decreasing as well. It is a delicate matter now- the Hawaiians trusting American businessmen. However, to be frank, we need your help. I'll let the good ambassador tell you of our hopes."

Thomas spoke up, "Gentlemen, I believe it would behoove California and Hawai'i to improve our trade relationships. We would like to meet with Mr. Blake and some of his farmers to discuss increasing sugar sales. We were thinking of an exchange of ideas. You could send some farmers to Hawai'i to improve our techniques, and we could send some farmers here to share our techniques."

Governor Markham leaned in, "That's a great idea. We also grow hay and alfalfa that could be used for your cattle. Plus grapes, apples, almonds, and tomatoes are all available to be part of the exchange."

David responded, "I have been told your city of Los Angeles wants to buy a thousand palm trees. We can sell you those."

The carriage stopped near a vehicle that King David thought looked like a small train that was attached to cables. The four men got out of their carriage.

Mayor Pond pointed to the cable car, "King David, we are going on a cable car ride! I think you will enjoy it. "This is the Pacific Avenue Cable Car. It will take us up this steep hill several blocks on Sutter Street and drop us off right in front of your hotel."

The cable car began to clang. The conductor rang the bell several times; the car slowly shook and began to move forward. It was an open-air car, which caused all of the dignitaries to act like young boys. The men swung off the car, holding on with one arm to the amusement of the people of San Francisco.

"I haven't had this much fun since I was a child!" David yelled. "Hang on tight Thomas! You won't be able to change diapers with a broken arm."

Thomas laughed, "And may I remind His Majesty that we need to bring him back to Hawai'i alive and in one piece?"

The four men and their police escort walked into *The Palace,* the finest hotel in San Francisco. King David walked into the opulent lobby and stopped suddenly. "Oh my! This is more beautiful than the Iolani Palace. This is a hotel?"

Mayor Pond, "Only the finest in San Francisco for His Majesty."

The rest of the entourage, along with several steamer trunks of the king's clothes, began to arrive.

Mayor Pond pointed to the elevator, "The Penthouse Suite and the entire floor is for you and your guests. The bellhops will bring your luggage in a moment. Have you ever been in an elevator before?"

"No Mayor. It appears to be a jail cell."

Oh I assure you that it's only for your safety. It will lift you up to your floor. Just leave it to the operator."

David was hesitant, but entered. The operator closed the door. David's eyes were wide with anticipation. The Hawaiians applauded as their king was hoisted up and out of view.

Keilani remarked, "What an amazing contraption Thomas."

Thomas quipped, "Indeed My Dear. These Americans sure can create the most amazing machines. I think it is time Hawai'i becomes more westernized. Don't you?"

"Oh Thomas, the king might want that, but Lydia loves the old ways. We will have to move slowly with her."

"Well I know you have influence with her, or maybe we need to bring her to San Francisco one day."

"Perhaps. OW!" Keilani screamed!

Thomas grabbed his wife by the shoulders to hold her up, "What's the matter Grace?"

She was bent over holding her side. "Oh it's gone now. But wow! It felt as if I was stabbed!"

"Are you sure you're ok?"

"Yes Thomas, let's ride this contraption up to the top floor."

King David spent several days in San Francisco. Californians came from all over the state to meet the king of Hawai'i and have a photograph taken with him. The king was the talk of the town.

Chapter 25
California Dreamin'
San Francisco, December 1890

The Kamehameha was scheduled to leave San Francisco on December 5. The itinerary was to sail down the coast of California to Los Angeles and San Diego in the hopes of increasing business opportunities between the kingdom of Hawai'i and California.

Thomas Baitmen ran up the gangplank as quickly as he could to talk to Captain Dale. "Captain, my wife is in labor. Can the ship wait until tomorrow to leave?"

Captain Dale replied, "That is entirely up to King David."

The ship's departure was already delayed due to difficulties Grace Keilani was having with her pregnancy. She was a few weeks early of her expected delivery date, December 25.

Ambassador Baitmen had become a trusted advisor to the king. Unfortunately, Thomas could not leave his wife in her time of difficulty. Thomas hurried down to the king's cabin.

"Your Majesty, I can't apologize enough for making you wait, but Grace is in labor, and I must stay with her!"

"Of course Thomas. Family first. I have several meetings scheduled, so we can't wait any longer. We will be back in a few weeks and we will take you, Grace Keilani, and your new baby back to Hawai'i with us. Please send her my love and we will be back soon."

"Thank you for understanding, Your Majesty." Thomas turned and scurried back to the taxi waiting to take him back to the hospital.

King David was saddened with Thomas' departure and looked at his guard Ka'le, "I just got a horrible feeling about Grace's condition. If anything were to happen to her, Lydia would be distraught."

Walter Blake was attending the voyage with the king. He made his way on board after receiving the news that *The Kamehameha* would set sail that day. "Your Majesty. I am looking forward to visiting Hawai'i and your sugar farms again next spring."

King David smiled. He had other things on his mind. David looked onto the bay from the deck as the winter sun set. It grew dark quickly. *The Kamehameha* slowly steamed out of the bay and passed a small island. The beam from the lighthouse of Alcatraz buzzed by and lit up the ship, "Walter, I truly hope our business deal can begin before I depart for Hawai'i next month. I can see it now," his hand slowly floated across the sky, "C & H sugar company! California and Hawai'i, the largest sugar company in the world. We will both be very rich men, don't you think?"

"Let's hope, Your Majesty! When you return, I will have that group of investors we talked about and begin looking for property for our plant. I think I know just the place. Its just a few miles boat ride into San Pablo Bay."

King David smiled, "I can't wait to meet them. Mahalo for everything. Aloha, Mr. Blake. I haven't been feeling myself today. I think I am going to my cabin to retire for the night."

The next day …

The Kamehameha sailed around the Farallon Islands. The king had been told of the massive elephant seals that lived on the islands for parts of the year. He was excited to see them.

Captain Dale Lathrop chimed in, "The monk seals of Hawai'i can get to be eight feet, but the male elephant seals can get to 20 feet long and weigh over 8,000 pounds!"

Captain Lathrop gave the king his binoculars. "Those elephant seals are enormous animals, Your Majesty. They are also quite a meal and attract the largest sharks in the world! They are called the great white sharks. They can be as large as whales!"

King David slowly lowered his binoculars and turned to the captain, "As large as whales?"

The captain said, "If the seals are here, the great whites are here too. Their mouths are so large they can swallow a man whole! I have seen them bite a six-foot seal in two before. LOOK! There's the dorsal fin of one right now about 50 yards from the island!"

King David watched through the binoculars as the shark approached a group of elephant seals swimming towards some rocks. Then as if to show off, the shark rose five feet straight out of the water with a baby seal in its mouth.

"So much blood." The king grimaced. "I am glad there are no great whites in Hawaiian waters. I would never go swimming."

The Kamehameha got back on course and headed south.

"The coastline seemed to go on forever." King David kept remarking as the trip went on for hours, "This state is so large."

Later that evening back in San Francisco.

Mayor Pond met with Thomas outside his flat. "Thomas, I think Grace needs to be transferred to Stanford Hospital. It's the best hospital in the country. I know a doctor there who is a great surgeon. His name is Doctor Jim Lions. He will take care of Grace. I have sent for an ambulance and you can get there in a couple hours."

By nightfall, Grace was admitted into the maternity ward. Thomas was in the waiting room and the surgeon came out to address the situation. "Mr Baitmen, Grace's pregnancy has complications. She has some internal bleeding, and the baby is a month premature. We are doing everything we can, but the baby might have to be delivered surgically. It might be the only way to save the mother and child. If you are a religious man, I suggest you pray."

Thomas got down on his knees and prayed for the safety of his family. He hadn't seen any of his siblings in a couple years due to his travels. He so wished they were here with him now instead of England. He had never felt so alone.

An hour later Doctor Lions walked through the door of the waiting room. He stopped and he looked down at the floor. Thomas stood up hopeful to hear some good news. His assistant, Doctor Faulkner walked over to Thomas, "Mr. Baitmen…. Grace had been hemorrhaging for longer than we believed. We needed to save the child as Grace's blood pressure crashed. We completed an emergency cesarean section. The baby is small, but otherwise in perfect health. Unfortunately Mr. Baitmen, your wife passed away a few minutes ago. You may go into surgery and spend some time with her. Your baby girl is in an incubator being attended to by the nurses. You may go see her when you are ready. I am so sorry for your loss."

Thomas fell to his knees and wept. Doctor Lions asked to get a nurse to help him get Thomas to his feet. The three staggered over to the operating room, and there Grace was. She looked like an angel peacefully sleeping. She had lost a little color but was beautiful nonetheless. Thomas kissed her forehead, cried, and asked Keilani, "What shall we call our baby girl?"

He stroked Grace's hair for a minute. "We will call her Maili. That means 'pebble' in Hawaiian. She will be the little pebble that came from such a strong rock of a mother. And of course, Grace will be her middle name. She will be named Maili Grace Baitmen Kaanapali."

The nurse gently said, "It's time to meet your daughter. Come with me." She pulled the sheet over Keilani's face. Thomas walked into the next room where the baby was lying in an incubator. Maili was a little ball swaddled in a pink blanket. Only her face moved as her mouth puckered and opened to a yawn. Lights above her were keeping her warm.

The nurse spoke softly, "I know this has been the worst night of your life, but your daughter needs you now more than you can imagine. We have this new milk called formula. It mimics mother's milk without having to breastfeed. Do you have anyone else to help you raise your daughter?"

Thomas continued to stare at Maili. "No" he said quietly. The king's ship left today with all of my friends."

"Mr. Baitmen, there are many deserving and childless parents who would be willing to raise your child," the nurse was trying to be helpful.

"No. I will raise my daughter the best that I can."

The nurse asked, "Do you have a name?"

"Yes. She will be called Maili Grace Baitmen Kaanapali." She was 15 inches long, and weighed 5 pounds 5 ounces.

Chapter 26
California Nightmare
Santa Barbara, California, January 19, 1891

The Kamehame had anchored off the coast of
Santa Barbara, California. Captain Lathrop
warned the king that February is often the
stormiest month in the Eastern Pacific, and if
they wanted to improve their chances of calm

seas, they needed to get back to San Francisco, pick up the Baitmens, and steam directly back to Pearl Harbor. The king had one last business dinner to attend before beginning the journey back.

King David was entertaining the local businessmen at a downtown restaurant. They were enjoying the fresh catch of the day, ling cod, octopus, scallops, crab, and the king's new favorite, king salmon.

"So gentlemen it's agreed, we will send a ship with pineapples, coffee, coconuts, and cut lava rock four times a year. You send us cattle, wheat, chickens, and some of that delicious king salmon."

The businessmen toasted, "CHEERS to King David and ALLOOOO HA!"

When the dinner ended and King David started to feel a little dizzy. He grabbed the table and Ka'le asked, "Are you ok, Your Majesty?"

"Oh I bet I just had a little too much of that Tennessee whisky." He tried to say with a smile, yet Ka 'le could see half of the king's face was frozen.

Ka'le got the attention of a local, "Please go get a doctor."

"Please sit down, Your Majesty. I believe something is wrong."

"I'm having… a little trouble speaking K kkkk a'le."

A doctor happened to be dining in the next room. In an instant he knew the king was having a stroke. "Let's get him to the hospital right away."

A patron with a motorcar drove he king a few blocks to the newly opened Santa Barbara Cottage Hospital.

A few moments later, the doctor who accompanied the king to the hospital addressed his entourage, "Gentlemen, I'm afraid the stroke is severe. I suggest you immediately take him to Stanford where they have the best doctors west of the Mississippi."

The next day, *The Kamehameha* steamed into San Francisco Bay. News of the tragedy spread throughout the city quickly. Thousands of the residents of San Francisco came out to mourn the king of Hawai'i's illness. The city had grown fond of the king.

The Stanford doctors did all they could, but King David passed away on January 20, 1891. The king was surrounded by his bodyguards, his close aide Kenneth Doel, Ambassador Baitmen, and baby Maili Grace. This would be one of the saddest days in San Francisco until 1906.

King David's body was placed in the most expensive coffin the city of San Francisco could purchase. A parade in the king's honor was lined with thousands of admirers. A low cloud cover filled the bay. The temperature dropped and the cold, wet air overwhelmed many of the onlookers. It appeared *Lilinoe*, the Hawaiian goddess of the rain and mist, made the trip across the mighty Pacific to mourn the loss of her king as well.

The Kamehameha left San Francisco Bay hosting the flag at half-staff.

The seas remained calm throughout the week-long voyage. Most of the crew remained silent during the voyage. The ship sailed through the Alenuihaha Channel, between Hawai'i and Maui. Captain Dale sailed as close as he could so the flag at half-staff could be seen. He could see the activity increase as he sailed past Kona. Dale wondered how Queen Emma would take the news. Would she try a coup? Dale later sailed around Maui near La Haina where Chief Kaanapali lived. Lastly they sailed around Moloka'i so the lepers of Kalaupapa could mourn.

From lookouts at Diamond and Koko Heads, word reached the Iolani Palace that the king's ship was returning. Princess Lydia was ecstatic. Her dear brother, the king, was returning. Lydia was also excited that returning would be her best friend Grace Keilani and her new baby.

Lydia dressed in a formal gown. She had been smiling all morning. Tavita walked up the stairs to greet the princess, but could not look at her. He did not speak. Lydia thought that this was quite unusual behavior for such a usually happy guy. In fact none of the guards spoke to her. They all remained at attention as the royal carriage rode down to Pearl Harbor. Her smile left. She began to wonder.

"Is there another coup about to happen?" She felt vulnerable.

As the carriage approached Pearl Harbor, the crowd that gathered on the streets was not cheering. They too would not look at the princess. They just looked at the ground. Many were crying. The princess stopped waving feeling it was inappropriate. She thought again, "I guess I'm going to die today. Well, I must be brave like Marie Antoinette!"

The carriage stopped at the edge of the water. The crowd remained silent. The guards were silent. She was determined to be brave, so she held her chin high and walked over to *The Kamehameha.* She looked on board and the crew had their hats off, yet still no one told her of the news of her brother and best friend.

A gust of wind hit her face and directed her attention to the mast. The flag was at half-staff. It all made sense now. She realized at that moment her brother was gone. Tears streamed down her face, yet she knew she needed to remain strong for her people. She took a deep breath through her nose and began to bravely march towards the ship.

Thomas Baitmen and Kenneth Doel approached her. Thomas could barely speak; he was so stricken with grief. "Princess Lydia, I am saddened to inform you that King David Kalākaua, your brother, passed away in San Francisco of complications from a stroke he had in Santa Barbara. I … am… so sorry, My Princess."

Lydia looked up in the sky. It was a cloudless day. The sky, the warm air, the turquoise bay could not have been more beautiful. However, very ugly thoughts filled her soul. "Who did this to David?" She demanded.

Kenneth spoke, between agonizing breaths, "The gods did, My Princess."

"I don't believe you! I bet it was the Americans!" She shouted to the gasps of the onlookers.

Thomas stepped back, "Please Lydia, there was no foul play." Then a woman Lydia had never seen before brought down a baby.

Between sobs, yet with pride, Thomas said, "May I introduce you to Maili Grace Baitmen Kaanapali."

Lydia was having difficulty grasping all that was happening. "Oh my, she is beautiful!" She said sweetly. Then she realized Keilani wasn't there, "But where is Keilani?"

Thomas began to wail. "I am so sorry, My Princess, but... Keilani died giving birth."

Lydia gave out a wail of grief that could be heard across the harbor. She staggered into Thomas' arms and passed out.

Lydia was lying in her bed at Iolani Palace. Sitting next to her and surrounding her bed were Kenneth and Mary Doel. Alongside them was their baby Elizabeth. Chief Kaanapali who was holding his granddaughter Maili, Queen Emma, and her bodyguard Sione were also there.

Lydia looked at Mary and Emma, "Is it true? Are our king and my sweet Keilani gone?"

Mary looked at Queen Emma. "Unfortunately my dear, your brother and best friend are with the ancestors now. As soon as you are ready, we have much to tell you, and to prepare for."

Chief Kaanapali softly spoke, "Princess Lydia, I am holding my granddaughter, Princess Maili. With my failing health, she will need a strong auntie to take care of her." With those words, he passed Maili to Lydia.

Lydia propped herself up in the bed. "Where is Thomas?"

The chief leaned in as Lydia settled Maili into her arms, "He received an urgent telegram. Apparently England is nearing war, and he was called home. Maili is too young for such a voyage, so we decided to keep her here in Hawai'i."

"How is Maili being fed?"

Mary spoke up, "There is this new invention called formula. It replicates mother's milk, so no need for a wet nurse. 'Progress' they say," she said with a smile.

Queen Emma stood and said sternly, "Princess Lydia, Chief Kaanapali and I have spoken, and we believe that is best for the future of Hawai'i…"

Lydia held tightly onto Maili.

"…that you become queen as soon as possible to thwart any thought that we are vulnerable. We have already alerted our militaries. Koa and Tafa will ready our troops here on O'ahu."

"Oh my! This day keeps getting more bizarre. A couple hours ago I was ready to meet my brother and best friend. They are dead. I have a new niece to raise, and I am to become queen. Any other devastating news?" She looked around the room.

Emma walked over to Lydia and placed something in her hand. "Thomas wanted me to make sure you got this back. He knew Keilani would want you to have it."

It was the necklace Lydia gave to Keilani years ago. Lydia just stared for a moment, then sobbed like a child.

Queen Emma responded, "Princess Lydia, if there is any woman strong enough to handle this, it would be you!"

The hurt and sadness in Lydia's eyes broke the hearts of everyone present. Lydia sniffed and took a huge breath. She pulled Baby Maili away to look into her big brown eyes as she drank from her bottle, "Well princess, you and I have much work to do. Hawai'i needs us to be strong. Let's get to work." Princess Maili smiled.

Made in United States
Troutdale, OR
01/15/2025

27627069R00156